RIDICULOUSLY COMPREHENSIVE DICTIONARY OF BRITISH SLANG

(Includes Cockney Rhyming Slang)

Compiled by Ian Hall

PHANTOM GAVEL PUBLICATIONS

Copyright © Ian Hall. Phantom Gavel Publications

Ian Hall is a member of the Phantom Gavel team.

ISBN-13: 978-1532949555

ISBN-10: 1532949553

All rights reserved, and the authors reserve the right to re-produce this book, or parts thereof, in any way whatsoever.

No part of this book may be reproduced or transmitted in any form or by any means, electronic or mechanical, including photocopying, recording, or by any information storage and retrieval system, without the written permission of the publisher, except where permitted by law.

RIDICULOUSLY COMPREHENSIVE DICTIONARY OF BRITISH SLANG

(Including English Slang, Scottish Slang, Irish Slang, Welsh Slang, Cockney Rhyming Slang, and Acronyms.)

Table of Contents

Introduction

A for Anorak

B for Belter

C for Ceilidh

D for Dog's Bollocks

E for Edgar Allen Poes

F for Flash Harry

G for Get Stuffed

H for Hand Shandy

I for InterCity

J for Jammies

K for Kecks

L for laughing Gear

M for Messages

N for Nutter

O for Oliver Hardy

P for Pissed as a Fart

Q for Quango

R for Right Little Earner

S for Sandy Lyle

T for Tom, Dick & Harry

U for Under the Cosh

V for VAT

W for Window Licker

Y for You're Having a Laugh

Z for Zachary Scotts

DISCLAIMER

Disclaimer.

Rude Words; I'm afraid there are rude words in this dictionary. If you read on from here, and are offended, it's your fault, you have been warned right from the start. I never set out to be rude, but I have to include these words in both the actual slang and in some definitions. Let's face it, people use rude words in slang, and some slang is used as an alternative for rude or foul words. I accept that some slang is downright bawdy and some ridiculously offensive, but again, make no apologies for its inclusion. So, take this warning, I don't know what level of rudeness you, the reader, wants, so I stuck it all in. Now, for everyone's benefit, I did throw an 'asterisk' into the middle of the two worst ones, but since slang is often used as an alternative to swear words, or to refer to certain words, I've kept it at a single 'asterisk'.

I hope you understand.

Alphabetical Order; This book has been written in fits and starts since I began the idea, a couple of years back. I am making no claims for the absolute perfect Oxford Alphabetical-ness of the individual definitions. I tried my best.

So if I made some small critical 'a-z' error, go bite me.

Anyway, I hope I can shed some light into the wacky morass we call slang, and provide both enlightenment and entertainment.

Ian Hall

INTRODUCTION

Our Purpose

It seems that while there are many decent British Slang dictionaries for sale, there appeared to be an overwhelming need for a GREAT one.

And that's what we did.

We decided to compile the super-updated, ridiculously comprehensive one!

Some alternative (and lesser) works are either old, outdated, badly written or downright short. So with our competitors' criteria in mind, we set to work.

We think we've covered the 'short' part by making our dictionary HUGE! With almost 200 pages of definition text, and over 4000 actual definitions... there's no cheesy filler... no huge explanatory chapters on the origins of slang; we all know where slang comes from! So we filled our pages with just definitions.

Yeah, I know it may seem a strange concept in a bleak universe, but we decided to offer value for money, not filler and lack of substance.

It's also totally up-to-date; there are slang references to internet, cell phones and President Obama. We also plan to update the dictionary a couple of times a year, and to that end we include our email address for you to send your favorite definition we've stupidly missed out.

(Email address is at the end of the book)

We've missed out some very basic terms, the ones that maybe only a letter or two differ from American English to British English; for instance, there'll be no adding

Aluminium (British; *Al-you-minni-um*) to

Aluminum (American; *Al-loo-min-um*)

to this dictionary… we just don't see the point.

What you get are definitions, and lots of them.

We've also covered Cockney Rhyming Slang to a great degree, and make no apologies for it. Cockney Rhyming Slang is becoming more popular, and we felt it needed a place to live and breathe. I've seen Dictionaries with just five pages of Cockney Rhyming Slang… we have hundreds and hundreds of Cockney definitions.

Slang

I have included three distinct 'slangs' in this dictionary; basic British slang, regional slang, and Cockney Rhyming slang. Each have their own origins, and their own idiosyncrasies.

Slang… has been around in every language from the beginning of time. Either by mis-speaking, or regional dialect, slang has grown into variable proportions in different countries. Every generation usually develop their own version of slang, each thinking they are unique in doing so.

Regional Slang… has been included in dialects and cadences. Each fraction of the British Isles has their own, and I have tried my best to include them all.

Cockney Rhyming Slang… is a rhyming method of speech (a secret language) first used and developed in the Cockney region of London. Initially meant for real secrets between crooks, villains, groups, etc, Cockney Rhyming Slang has spread in varying degrees to the whole of the UK and beyond.

Cockney Rhyming Slang has three distinct variations, each rarer than the other…

1st degree Cockney Rhyming Slang… By far the most commonly heard and used (when the rhyme is essential).

Example; "He went up the Apples and Pears."

Meaning… He went up the stairs.

(Cockney Rhyming Slang for 'stairs', is 'Apples and Pears')

2nd degree Cockney Rhyming Slang… Rarely heard and spoken (when the rhyming part has been dropped)…

Example; "He kicked me in the Alberts!"

Meaning… He kicked me in the testicles (balls).

(Cockney Rhyming Slang for testicles (balls) is 'Albert Halls', but in this case the rhyming part ('Halls') is dropped, leaving the user with a brand new slang term)

3rd degree Cockney Rhyming Slang... Very rare. When the original rhyme has been dropped, and the other part of the original phrase has also been dropped, to be replaced by another word associated with it.

Example; "Calm down, mate, keep your Elvis."

Meaning... keep your hair on.

(Cockney Rhyming Slang for 'hair-on' is Aaron. But the original Aaron has been dropped being replaced by Elvis, an obvious associated word, although 'Elvis' was never in the original rhyming slang.)

The Old British Monetary System

Despite my urgent need to get on to the definitions, I feel it only right to waffle just a little about the old British monetary system before it went decimal in 1971. Hopefully this will shed some light on the coins and terms of the dictionary definitions which deal with 'old-money'; Pounds, Shillings and pennies.

Farthing Coin - Quarter of a penny, used until 1960.

Halfpenny Coin – Half a penny, used until 1971.

Penny Coin – A penny, large copper coin, twelve pennies made a shilling. 240 pennies made a pound.

Threepence Coin – Threepence coin, usually called a 'thruppeny bit', it was thick and twelve sided. Four thruppences made a shilling.

Sixpence Coin – Six penny coin, small thin, silver colored. Two sixpences made a shilling.

Shilling Coin – Usually called a 'bob', or 'one bob bit'. Twenty shillings made a pound.

Two Shilling Coin – Yup, this was called a 'two bob bit', or a florin.

Half Crown Coin – This is where it gets slightly confusing. This is a two and a half shilling coin. It helps in this case to think American; the half-crown is actually a quarter of a pound.

Crown Coin – rarely used in service, mostly for commorative issues.

(I hope the above made sense.)

No More Waffle

Okay, the introduction's over, let's get on with the actual dictionary. Over 180 pages of definitions.

We love you all, and hope you have a great time.

A IS FOR ANORAK

AA – Automobile Association, like triple A (AAA).

A & E – Accident & Emergency (Emergency Room)

A and B the C of D – Above and Beyond the Call of Duty.

Abbatoir – Slaughterhouse for animals.

Aberdonian – Person from Aberdeen, Scotland.

Abergavenny - Cockney Rhyming Slang for 'Penny'.

Abin – Scottish for 'above'.

A Bit of a Do – An understatement of a really big party, bash, occasion.

A Bit on the Side – Having a romantic liaison as well as your regular relationship.

Able and Willing – Cockney Rhyming Slang for 'Shilling'. Also 2nd Degree CRS on the word 'Able'. "Lend me an Able, I'm broke!"

Abnab – Liverpool for 'sandwich'.

Aboon – Scottish for 'above'.

Aboot – Scottish for 'about'.

Absobloodyutely – Absolutely with 'bloody' inserted in the middle; with certainty, completely.

Ace - If something is ace it is awesome; cool, ace brill, brilliant.

Ace in the Hole – A hidden/secret advantage.

Ace of Spades – Cockney Rhyming Slang for 'Aids'.

Ache and Pain - Cockney Rhyming Slang for 'Rain'.

Ack Ack – Short for 'anti-aircraft', from WW1.

Acker Bilk - Cockney Rhyming Slang for 'Milk'. (origins; he was a 60's band leader and clarinetist)

Ackers – Liverpool for 'money'.

Ackle – To work properly, as intended.

Action Man – British version of GI-Joe.

Adam and Eve – Cockney Rhyming Slang for 'believe'. Eg; "Would you Adam and Eve it?"

Adam and the Ants - Cockney Rhyming Slang for 'Pants'. (trousers)

Adam Faith - Cockney Rhyming Slang for 'Safe'. "Let's put our valuables in the Adam Faith!" (origins; he was a 60's British singer/actor)

Addled – Drunk, disorientated, acting silly.

Adrian Mole - Cockney Rhyming Slang for 'Dole'. (Social Security) (origins; he was a youth book/TV character)

Aerial – A UK word for a TV or radio antenna.

Afters – Pudding, desert, the sweet after your 'meat and potatoes' meal.

Age Before Beauty – Sarcastic phrase to mock someone, usually an elder. "You go first... age before beauty."

Aggro - Short for aggravation, it's the sort of thing you might expect at a football match. In other words - trouble! There is sometimes aggro in the cities after the pubs shut!

Agriculture Show – UK version of a state fair... where farmers go to show off their prize animals and look at the latest tractors.

Air Biscuit – A fart.

Air Pie and Windy Pudding – Nothing to eat.

Air Miles - Cockney Rhyming Slang for 'Piles'. (Hemorrhoids)

Airs and Graces - Cockney Rhyming Slang for 'Braces'. (Suspenders)

AJ Hackett - Cockney Rhyming Slang for 'Jacket'.

A La Mode - Cockney Rhyming Slang for 'Code'. "Hey, henry, we've got to talk a la mode, behind the school".

Al Capone - Cockney Rhyming Slang for 'telephone'.

Al Caponed - Cockney Rhyming Slang for 'stoned'. (drunk)

Alcopop – A bottled fizzy drink containing alcohol.

All Day-er – A job, task, or drinking session, lasting all day.

Alley Apple – Stone, pebble.

All Fur Coat and No Knickers – A description of a classy lady who has loose morals, or all style and no substance.

All Mod Cons – Having the most modern design, an abbreviation of 'all modern conveniences'.

All Mouth and No Trousers – No substance, a person who acts with bravado, but fails to live up his own hype.

All Nighter – A job, task, or drinking session lasting all night.

All Over the Shop – All over the place, or all over the map, all round the house. Disorganised, in a mess.

All Piss and Wind - No substance, a person who acts with bravado, but fails to live up to his own hype.

All right? – Sometimes thought of as a "Hello, how are you?", it is also just a general greeting of "hello", sometimes answered back in the same manner.

Allus – Yorkshire for 'always'.

Al Pachino - Cockney Rhyming Slang for 'Cappuchino'.

Alan Border - Cockney Rhyming Slang for 'out of order'. (origins; he was an English cricketer)

Alan Knott - Cockney Rhyming Slang for 'hot'. (origins; he was an English cricketer)

Alan Ladd - Cockney Rhyming Slang for 'bad'. (origins; he was an American actor)

Alan Minter - Cockney Rhyming Slang for both 'printer' or 'splinter'. (origins; he was an English Boxer)

Alan Pardew - Cockney Rhyming Slang for 'Flu'. (origins; he is an English football manager)

Alan Whicker(s) - Cockney Rhyming Slang for both a 'nicker' (British pound) and 'knickers'. (origins; he was a famous English TV personality)

Albert Hall(s) - Cockney Rhyming Slang for 'balls'. (testicles) 2nd degree Cockney Rhyming Slang…(when the rhyming part has been dropped)… "He kicked me in the Alberts!"

Alex Nash - Cockney Rhyming Slang for 'slash'. (urinate)

Alfie Moon - Cockney Rhyming Slang for 'coon'. (a person of black colour)

Alger Hiss - Cockney Rhyming Slang for 'piss'.

Ali Mcgraw - Cockney Rhyming Slang for 'score'. 2nd degree Cockney Rhyming Slang…(when the rhyming part has been dropped)… "What's the Ali, mate?"

Alibi Ike - Cockney Rhyming Slang for 'bike'.

Alice Bands - Cockney Rhyming Slang for 'hands'.

All Behind - Cockney Rhyming Slang for 'blind'.

All Night Rave - Cockney Rhyming Slang for 'shave'.

All Time Looser - Cockney Rhyming Slang for 'boozer'. (bar, pub)

Almond Rocks - Cockney Rhyming Slang for 'socks'.

Alphonse - Cockney Rhyming Slang for 'ponce'.

Amber Nectar – Yellow (golden) lager.

Anall – Yorkshire for 'and all'. Me too. As well.

Anchor Spreadable - Cockney Rhyming Slang for 'incredible'.

Ancient Greek - Cockney Rhyming Slang for both 'reek' and 'freak'.

And No Mistake – Undoubtedly, absolutely, for certain. Usually used as a last remark.

Andy Farley - Cockney Rhyming Slang for 'charlie' (cocaine).

Andy McNab(s) - Cockney Rhyming Slang for both 'cab', 'crabs' and kebab'.

Andy Pandy - Cockney Rhyming Slang for both 'dandy', and brandy'. (origins; British children's TV character)

Anekka Rice - Cockney Rhyming Slang for 'price'. (origins; British TV personality)

Angela Merkel - Cockney Rhyming Slang for 'circle'.

Angus MacGyver - Cockney Rhyming Slang for 'skiver'.

Ann Boleyn - Cockney Rhyming Slang for 'gin'. 2nd degree Cockney Rhyming Slang…(when the rhyming part has been dropped)… "You have a beer, I'll have an Ann."

Ann Frank - Cockney Rhyming Slang for 'wank'.

Annie May Wong - Cockney Rhyming Slang for 'strong'. 2nd degree Cockney Rhyming Slang…(when the rhyming part has been dropped)… "That cheese is a bit Annie May!"

Anorak – Initially a waterproof jacket. Sometimes used to describe a geek, nerd, obsessed with one subject. Train spotters wear anoraks.

Answerphone – A phone recording device.

Anti-clockwise – Counter-clockwise,(Nothing against clocks!).

Ant and Dec(s) - Cockney Rhyming Slang for 'cheque', or 'oral sex'. (origins; British TV personalities)

Anthea Turner - Cockney Rhyming Slang for 'earner'.

Anthony Blunt - Cockney Rhyming Slang for 'c*nt'.

Anti-Septic – 2nd Degree Cockney Rhyming Slang for 'anti-American'. From 'Septic Tank- 'yank'.

Antwacky – Old fashioned.

Any Road (up) – Yorkshire for 'anyway'.

Apple Bobbing - Cockney Rhyming Slang for 'robbing'.

Apple Cider - Cockney Rhyming Slang for 'spider'.

Apple Core - Cockney Rhyming Slang for 'score'.

Apple Fritter - Cockney Rhyming Slang for both 'bitter', and 'shitter' (arse).

Apple Pie - Cockney Rhyming Slang for 'sky'.

Apples and Oranges – Used to point out the distinct differences between two items that are similar to begin with.

Apples and Pears – Cockney Rhyming Slang for 'stairs'.

April Fool(s) - Cockney Rhyming Slang for both 'fool', 'pools', and 'stools'.

April in Paris - Cockney Rhyming Slang for 'arse'.

April Showers - Cockney Rhyming Slang for 'flowers'.

Arabian Nights - Cockney Rhyming Slang for 'shites'.

Arethusa - Cockney Rhyming Slang for 'boozer'.

Argy Bargy – Slang for an 'argument', disagreement, or even a fist fight.

A Right Carry-On – Slang for a bit of a mess, disorganized, shambolic.

Aristotle - Cockney Rhyming Slang for 'bottle'. (guts, courage)

Army and Navy - Cockney Rhyming Slang for 'gravy'.

Arnold Palmer - Cockney Rhyming Slang for 'farmer'. (origins; American golfer)

Arrows – Darts; the game played in bars.

Arse - UK-speak for 'ass'. So 'half-arsed' means 'half-assed'.

Arse About Face - This means you are doing something back to front; the wrong way round.

Arse Antlers – Tattoo on a woman's back, just above her arse.

Arse End of Nowhere – A remote location. In the middle of nowhere.

Arse Over Elbow - Fall over dramatically, rolling.

Arse Over Tit - Another version of arse over elbow, but a bit more graphic!

Arsehole - Assholes to you Americans. Not a nice word in either language.

Arseholed - Drunk! Usually in the advanced stages of drunken stupor, someone would be considered "completely arseholed". Never me, of course!

Artful Dodger - Cockney Rhyming Slang for 'lodger'.

Arthur Ashe - Cockney Rhyming Slang for 'slash'. 2nd degree Cockney Rhyming Slang…(when the rhyming part has been dropped)… "Nipping round the back for an Arthur."

Arthur Conan Doyle - Cockney Rhyming Slang for 'boil'. 2nd degree Cockney Rhyming Slang…(when the rhyming part has been dropped)… "Get that kettle on the Arthur, I'm parched!".

ASBO – Anti Social Behavior Order.

As the Actress said to the Bishop – A weird expression from music hall days, usually said after a deliberate double-entendre expression to emphasize the rude meaning.

As Well - Means 'also' or 'too'. "You're having a lemon cake? I'll have one as well."

As Much Use as a Chocolate Fireguard – No use whatsoever, completely useless.

As Welcome as a Fart in a Spacesuit – Not welcome at all, very unwanted.

Ass - Your backside, rump, but also a donkey.

Atilla the Hun - Cockney Rhyming Slang for '2-1', a football score.

At It – On the con, on the take, poking fun, a general expression towards a questionable character.

At Sixes and Sevens – In a mixed-up state, not organized.

At the Sharp End – Working at the dangerous end of an operation. "The troops at the front-line; they're at the sharp end".

Aubergine – Eggplant.

Au Fait - To be 'okay' or familiar with something.

Auld – Scottish for 'old'.

Auld Reekie – Old name for Edinburgh, Scotland.

Auntie (beeb) – A quaint word for the BBC. (British Broadcasting Corporation) Beeb is another.

Aunt Mabel - Cockney Rhyming Slang for 'table'.

Aunt Nell - Cockney Rhyming Slang for 'smell', and 'bell'..

Aunt Ella - Cockney Rhyming Slang for 'umbrella'.

Auntie Nellie - Cockney Rhyming Slang for 'belly', or 'telly' (television)

Austin Power - Cockney Rhyming Slang for 'shower'.

Auxters - A Mis-spelling of Oxters, ie; armpits.

Avvy – Liverpool for afternoon.

Away – In prison.

Ayers Rock - Cockney Rhyming Slang for 'cock', (penis).

Aylesbury Duck - Cockney Rhyming Slang for 'f*ck'. 2nd degree Cockney Rhyming Slang…(when the rhyming part has been dropped)… "Sorry mate, I don't give an Aylesbury!"

Ayrton Senna - Cockney Rhyming Slang for 'tenner'. (origins; racing driver)

B IS FOR BELTER

B in the D – Back in the Day.

Baa Lamb - Cockney Rhyming Slang for 'tram'.

Babbling Brook - Cockney Rhyming Slang for 'crook'.

Babe Magnet – Something/someone that has the ability/power to attract women.

Babe Ruth - Cockney Rhyming Slang for 'truth'.

Bacardi Breezer - Cockney Rhyming Slang for 'geezer', also 'freezer'.

Baccy - Short for Tobacco. Commonly the sort you use to roll your own.

Back and Front - Cockney Rhyming Slang for 'c*nt'.

Back Benches – Being in parliament, but not having a committee or post position.

Back End of a Bus – Ugly person.

Back Green – The grass behind your house (Scottish)

Back of (time) – Just, or minutes after. "I'll meet you, back of ten". ('I'll meet you, 5 or ten minutes after ten')

Back of Beyond – A remote location. In the middle of nowhere.

Back to Front - Cockney Rhyming Slang for 'c*nt'.

Backy – Giving a (second) person a ride on the back of a bike.

Bacon and Eggs - Cockney Rhyming Slang for 'legs'.

Bacon Bits - Cockney Rhyming Slang for 'tits'.

Bacon Bonce - Cockney Rhyming Slang for 'nonce'.

Bacon Butty - Cockney Rhyming Slang for 'nutty'.

Bacon Rind - Cockney Rhyming Slang for 'mind', also 'blind'.

Bacon Sarnie - Cockney Rhyming Slang for 'Pakistani'.

Bad – Good. (How did that ever start?)

Bad Egg – Bad person.

Bad Job – Bad luck, hard lines.

Baffies – Slippers. (Scotland)

Bag For Life - Cockney Rhyming Slang for 'wife'.

Bag of Fruit - Cockney Rhyming Slang for 'suit'.

Bag of Sand - Cockney Rhyming Slang for '1000 pounds, or a grand'.

Bag of Yeast - Cockney Rhyming Slang for 'beast', also 'priest'.

Bagsie (Bagsy) – A children's expression to claim something. "I bagsie first go on the swings!"

Bahookie – Bum, bottom. (Scottish)

Bail (Bale) of Hay - Cockney Rhyming Slang for 'gay'.

Bairn – Scottish for child (east).

Baked Bean - Cockney Rhyming Slang for 'Queen'.

Baked Beans - Cockney Rhyming Slang for 'jeans'.

Baked Potato - Cockney Rhyming Slang for 'see ya later'.

Balaclava – A knitted hood, as worn by commandoes, or by skiers or those in cold conditions.

Bald as a Coot – A coot has no hair (it has feathers).

Bale of Straw - Cockney Rhyming Slang for 'raw'.

Ball and Bat - Cockney Rhyming Slang for 'twat'.

Ballet Dancer - Cockney Rhyming Slang for 'chancer'.

Ball of Chalk - Cockney Rhyming Slang for 'walk'.

Balloon Car - Cockney Rhyming Slang for 'saloon bar'.

Balls-Up – A total mess of things.

Baltic - Really cold. (Scottish)

Bambi and Thumper - Cockney Rhyming Slang for 'trumper', an arsehole.

Bamboo Shoots - Cockney Rhyming Slang for 'boots'.

Bampot – Scottish for an idiot, a person having little sense, but no idea of his shortcomings.

Bananarama - Cockney Rhyming Slang for 'drama. (Source, English pop group)

Band in the Box - Cockney Rhyming Slang for 'the pox'.

Band of Hope - Cockney Rhyming Slang for 'soap'.

Bang - To have sex.

Banged Up – Many meanings… In prison, locked up… pregnant (the result of a bang)… injured in a fight.

Banger – Firework that just goes bang. (Scottish)

Bangers – Sausages. Women's breasts.

Bangers and Mash – Sausages, and mashed potatoes, usually with brown (beef) gravy.

Bangers and Mash - Cockney Rhyming Slang for 'trash', 'cash', also 'slash' (pee).

Bang Goes Sixpence – Throwing money away on a bad purchase.

Banging – excellent, good, loud.

Bang Out of Order – Something or someone that is very wrong, has gone too far... way too far in a situation.

Bang to Rights – Caught red-handed. To be found/know you are guilty.

Banjaxed – Confused, disorientated.

Bap(s) – Bread rolls. Women's Breasts

Barack Obama's - Cockney Rhyming Slang for 'pyjamas'.

Barb Wired - Cockney Rhyming Slang for 'tired'.

Barclay's Bank - Cockney Rhyming Slang for 'wank'.

Bargain Hunt - Cockney Rhyming Slang for 'c*nt'.

Barking Mad – One stage above mad.

Barking Up the Wrong Tree – To be wrong about something, misled, mistaken.

Barmy – Mad, crazy.

Barnaby Rudge - Cockney Rhyming Slang for 'judge'.

Barnet Fair - Cockney Rhyming Slang for 'hair'.

Barney – A fight, an argument, fist-fight.

Barney Marlin - Cockney Rhyming Slang for 'darlin''.

Barney Rubble - Cockney Rhyming Slang for 'trouble', also 'double'.

Bar of Soap - Cockney Rhyming Slang for 'Pope'.

Barra – A small child, (Scottish), a wheelbarrow (North English).

Barrister – An attorney, usually in wig and robes in court.

Barry – Great, good, fantastic.

Barry Brown - Cockney Rhyming Slang for 'frown'.

Barry Cluff - Cockney Rhyming Slang for 'rough'.

Barry Crocker - Cockney Rhyming Slang for 'shocker'.

Barry McGuigan - Cockney Rhyming Slang for 'biggun'.

Barry Nash - Cockney Rhyming Slang for 'slash' (pee).

Barry White - Cockney Rhyming Slang for 'shite'.

Basement Jaxx - Cockney Rhyming Slang for 'tracks'.

Bash the Bishop – Yet another euphemism for male masturbation.

Basil Brush - Cockney Rhyming Slang for 'thrush'.

Basil Fawlty - Cockney Rhyming Slang for 'balti'. (Balti is a style of Indian Curry)

Basket – The front bulge in a man's trousers.

Bat and Ball - Cockney Rhyming Slang for 'tall'.

Bat and Wicket - Cockney Rhyming Slang for 'ticket'.

Baths (The) - Short for 'The Swimming Baths'. The local pool (Usually indoors in the UK).

Bath Tub - Cockney Rhyming Slang for 'pub'.

Bathroom Tap - Cockney Rhyming Slang for 'Jap'.

Bathroom Tiles - Cockney Rhyming Slang for 'piles'.

Battleaxe – A terrifying woman, usually old but not limited to.

Battle Cruiser - Cockney Rhyming Slang for 'boozer', (pub).

Battle of Waterloo - Cockney Rhyming Slang for 'stew'.

Bawhair – Very small measurement, usually the width of a pubic hair. (Scottish) "Aye, move it closer… just a bawhair!"

Baws – Testicles. (Scottish)

Bawbag – Scrotum bag. (Scottish) Used derogatively.

Bawbee – Old Scottish penny.

Baydon Powell - Cockney Rhyming Slang for 'trowel'. (Source, he invented the Scout movement)

Bazaar - Cockney Rhyming Slang for 'bar'.

Beak – Nose.

Beam Me Up Scotty - Cockney Rhyming Slang for 'Totty'. Nice looking women.

Beans on Toast - Cockney Rhyming Slang for 'post'. (mail)

Beans on Toast – Also called the Student's Lunch'. A delicacy.

Bear's Paw - Cockney Rhyming Slang for 'saw'.

Beastly – Nasty, unpleasant.

Beating Heart - Cockney Rhyming Slang for 'tart'.

Beautiful Game – Football; don't even think of calling it soccer. The whole world (except USA) calls it Football

Beaver Away – To work at something, head down, concentrating, ignoring everything else.

Becks & Posh - Cockney Rhyming Slang for 'nosh'. (Food) (Source, David Beckham & Posh Spice)

Beeb – The BBC.

Beefeaters – The costumed soldiers that 'guard' the Tower of London.

Bee Hive - Cockney Rhyming Slang for 'drive'.

Beecham's Pill - Cockney Rhyming Slang for 'pill' or 'still'.

Bees and Honey - Cockney Rhyming Slang for 'money'.

Bees Knees – Very good. A great example/version of something.

Bees Wax - Cockney Rhyming Slang for 'tax'.

Beef Curtains - Very slang term for a woman's labia.

Beer Ears – Alcohol induced hearing that makes bad music sound good.

Beer Glasses/Goggles/Spectacles – Alcohol enhanced property that makes ugly people look beautiful.

Beggar Belief – Staggers the imagination.

Beggar Boy's Arse - Cockney Rhyming Slang for 'Brass'. (Prostitute) or 'Bass' (guitar).

Beggar My Neighbour - Cockney Rhyming Slang for 'Labour (Exchange) (Unemployed, Dole)

Behind With The Rent - Cockney Rhyming Slang for 'Bent'.

Believe You Me – Means "I tell you" in the middle of a sentence.

Belinda Carlisle's - Cockney Rhyming Slang for 'Piles'. (Hemorroids)

Belter – Great, fantastic. (Scottish)

Bell – To call someone on the phone. "I'll give you a bell on Sunday".

Bell End - A stupid person, annoying, irritating.

Bell Ringers - Cockney Rhyming Slang for 'fingers'.

Belt Buckle - Cockney Rhyming Slang for 'chuckle'.

Belter – Means 'a real good one' in so many ways. "She's my girl, she's a belter." "He walked up to the football and kicked it, oh what a belter."

Belt up – As kids we heard this a lot. It's British for shut up.

Ben – Scottish for mountain.

Ben – Scottish, go through, or down. "Get ben the scullery." "Go through to the kitchen".

Ben Cartwright - Cockney Rhyming Slang for 'shite'.

Bender - A gay man, or pub crawl; a heavy drinking session.

Bended Knees - Cockney Rhyming Slang for 'cheese'.

Ben Dover - Cockney Rhyming Slang for 'hangover'.

Bendy Flex - Cockney Rhyming Slang for 'sex'.

Bengal Lancer - Cockney Rhyming Slang for 'chancer'.

Benny Hills - Cockney Rhyming Slang for 'pills'. Also 2nd degree Cockney Rhyming Slang; "I'm going to get Benny'd up" (Take some pills)

Ben Sherman - Cockney Rhyming Slang for 'German'.

Bent – Many meanings… gay… out of shape… weird… criminal… stolen.

Bent as a Three Bob watch – Very dodgy, a fraud, a forgery.

Bent as a Nine Bob Note – Homosexual or corrupt, illegal, a forgery.

Berk – An idiot, but not meant in a nasty way.

Berkshire Hunt - Cockney Rhyming Slang for 'c*nt'.

Bernard Langer - Cockney Rhyming Slang for 'banger'. (Sausage). (Source, German golfer)

Bernard Matthew - Cockney Rhyming Slang for 'queue'. (Source, English Chicken manf.)

Bernard Miles - Cockney Rhyming Slang for 'piles)

Bernie Flint - Cockney Rhyming Slang for 'skint'. (broke). (Source, English pop singer)

Bernie Winter - Cockney Rhyming Slang for 'printer'. (Source, English comedian)

Besom – Scottish for broom, or a difficult woman. "Bissum".

Best of British - If someone says "The best of British to you" when you are visiting the UK, it simply means good luck. It is short for "best of British luck".

Bethnal Greens - Cockney Rhyming Slang for 'jeans'.

Better Off Dead - Cockney Rhyming Slang for 'red'. (Communist)

Better than a Poke in the Eye with a Sharp Stick – Better than nothing.

Betty Boo - Cockney Rhyming Slang for 'poo'. 2nd degree Cockney Rhyming Slang: "I'm bursting for a Betty."

Betty Grable - Cockney Rhyming Slang for 'table'.

Bevvied – Drunk, having had quite a few.

Bevvy – Alcoholic drink of any kind.

Bexley Heath - Cockney Rhyming Slang for 'teeth'.

Bib & Brace - Cockney Rhyming Slang for 'face'.

Biccie/Bikky – Biscuit, a cookie.

Bide – Stay, live. (Scottish)

Big Ben - Cockney Rhyming Slang for 'ten'.

Big Dippers - Cockney Rhyming Slang for 'slippers'.

Biggie – A number two, a shit, or erection.

Big E, The - Short for 'The Elbow'. Giving someone the 'elbow' means 'getting rid of of them, or sacking/firing them'.

Big Girl's Blouse – An effeminate man or boy.

Bill – In bars and restaurants, this means your 'ticket', also a shortened version of 'Old Bill'; police.

Bill & Ben - Cockney Rhyming Slang for 'ten', or 'pen'. (Source, UK Kids show)

Bill & Benner - Cockney Rhyming Slang for 'tenner'. (Source, UK Kids show)

Bill Murray - Cockney Rhyming Slang for 'curry'. (Source, USA comedian)

Bill Oddie - Cockney Rhyming Slang for 'Voddy'. (Vodka.) (Source, English comedian)

Bill Roffie - Cockney Rhyming Slang for 'coffee'.

Billie Piper - Cockney Rhyming Slang for 'windscreen wiper', or 'sniper', or 'hyper'. (Source, English actress)

Billy Bunter - Cockney Rhyming Slang for 'punter'. (Source, UK comic character)

Billy Goat - Cockney Rhyming Slang for 'throat'.

Billy Hunt - Cockney Rhyming Slang for 'silly c*nt'.

Billy No (Nae) Mates – A beautiful description of a person with no friends.

Billy Ray Cyrus - Cockney Rhyming Slang for 'virus'. (Source, USA singer)

Bin Laden - Cockney Rhyming Slang for 'garden'.

Bin Lid – Cockney Rhyming Slang for 'kids'.. (Source, English comedian) Also colloquial for a hat.

Bin - Short for 'Rubbish/Trash Bin'. Also spectacles, glasses.

Bint – A slightly derogatory word for girlfriend, or female companion.

Bird – A woman, young girl.

Bird Bath - Cockney Rhyming Slang for 'laugh'.

Bird Lime - Cockney Rhyming Slang for 'time'.

Bird's Nest - Cockney Rhyming Slang for 'chest'.

Birl – Spin. (Scottish)

Biro - Short for 'Ballpoint Pen'. Lazlo Biro was the Hungarian Inventor.

Biscuit & Cookie - Cockney Rhyming Slang for 'bookie, rookie, or nookie'.

Biscuits and Cheese - Cockney Rhyming Slang for 'knees'.

Bish Bash Bosh - Cockney Rhyming Slang for 'wash'.

Bishy Barnaby – Ladybird.

Bisto – Brand of gravy granules.

Bit o' Luck - Cockney Rhyming Slang for 'luck'.

Bitter – Brown beer.

Bits and Bobs/Bats – Various little things, assorted objects. "On a desert Island, I'd survive with my pack of bits and bobs."

Bit of a Do – A fancy party.

Bit on the Side – An extra-marital partner, usually a secret.

Bizzies – Liverpool for the 'police'.

Black & Decker - Cockney Rhyming Slang for 'pecker'.

Black as the Earl of Hell's Waistcoat – My dad's way of saying 'very black'. A very dark skinned person.

Black as Newgate's Knocker – Very black. (Newgate was a prison)

Blackpool Rock - Cockney Rhyming Slang for 'cock'.

Blackpool Tower - Cockney Rhyming Slang for 'shower'.

Bladdered - This rather ugly expression is another way of saying you are drunk… your bladder is full.

Blade of Grass - Cockney Rhyming Slang for 'arse'.

Blackleg – A person who breaks a strike.

Blag – To rob, steal or trick your way into something. A robbery. To get by deception.

Blagger – A liar.

Blast - An exclamation of surprise. You may also hear someone shout "blast it", or even "bugger and blast"! Also means great fun; "I'm having a blast!"

Blatant - We use this word a lot to mean something is really obvious.

Blood Red - Cockney Rhyming Slang for 'head'.

Bloody Mary - Cockney Rhyming Slang for 'hairy'.

Bleb – Yorkshire for 'blister'.

Bleeding - An alternative to the curse word 'bloody'. You'll hear people say "bleeding hell" or "not bleeding likely" for example.

Blether – To talk a lot, talk nonsense. A person who can't seem to shut up.

Blighter – A scallywag, a scoundrel.

Blighty – Britain.

Blinder – Means you've 'played well', or 'worked well'. "I watched Jimmy in the team last night, he played a blinder."

Blimey - An exclamation of surprise. My Dad used to say "Gawd Blimey" or "Gor Blimey" or even "Cor Blimey". It is all a corruption of the oath "God Blind Me".

Blinding – Awesome. "The fete was a blinding success."

Blinkered - Someone who is blinkered is narrow minded or narrow sighted - they only see one view on a subject. Like blinkers used on a horse to restrict sideways looks.

Blitzed – Very Drunk.

Bloater – A fat person.

Block of Flats – Means a tall accommodation building; a Skyscraper.

Bloke – A man.

Bloody - One of the most useful swear words in English. Mostly used as an exclamation of surprise i.e. "bloody hell" or "bloody Nora". Something may be "bloody Marvellous" or "bloody awful". It is also used to emphasise almost anything, "you're bloody mad", "not bloody likely" and can also be used in the middle of other words to emphasise them. E.g. "Abso-bloody-lutely"! Americans should avoid saying "bloody" as they sound silly.

Bloody Nora – Another way to say 'Oh my Goodness'.

Blooming - Another alternative to the word bloody. You might hear someone say "not blooming likely" so that they don't have to swear.

Blootered – Yet another word to explain being very drunk. I'm sure we have 100 of these, just like Eskimo's have lots of words for snow.

Blot Your Copybook – To commit a crime/mistake/gaffe that spoils your record.

Blotto – Very drunk.

Blow off – Fart.

Blower – Telephone.

Blow me – Expression which means "well I never!"

Blue Peter - Cockney Rhyming Slang for 'heater'.

Blunt – 'Not sharp', as in knife.

Boak – to be sick, or to make someone feel sick. "You're givin' me the boak!"

Boat Race - Cockney Rhyming Slang for 'face'.

Boba Fett - Cockney Rhyming Slang for 'wet'.

Bob – A shilling.

Bobbins and Cotton - Cockney Rhyming Slang for 'rotten'.

Bobby Brown - Cockney Rhyming Slang for 'town'.

Bobby Dazzler – A cracker! Really good-looking person.

Bob Dylan - Cockney Rhyming Slang for 'villain'.

Bobby Moore - Cockney Rhyming Slang for 'sure'. (Source, English footballer)

Bobby – A policeman.

Bob Cryer - Cockney Rhyming Slang for 'liar'. (Source, English comedian)

Bob Hope - Cockney Rhyming Slang for 'dope'. (drugs) (Source, USA comedian)

Bob Marley - Cockney Rhyming Slang for 'charlie'. (cocaine)

Bob's Your Uncle – There it is, done, QED!

Bodge – To make a mess of, not do it properly.

Boffin – A person who has a technical job of some note, a scientist, mathematician, etc.

Bog – One of the various ways to say 'Toilet'.

Bogging – Scottish slang for crappy, rotten.

Bog Roll – Toilet roll, Bath tissue.

Bog Standard – The Basic version of something. Nothing out of the ordinary.

Bogey - Booger. Any variety of solid infestation of the nostrils, crusty dragons included!

Boiler – Is a girlfriend (or boyfriend) who's not that nice to look at. Kinda ugly.

Bollocks – No good, rubbish, also testicles.

Bolshy – Having an attitude, being difficult to work with, having a chip on your shoulder (from Bolshevik or Socialist).

Bomb - Really expensive, or really good, top quality. Going really well or really fast. "It's the bomb".

Bona Fide – Usually meaning, genuine, without hint of deceit or cheating.

Bombay Belly (Tummy) – An upset stomach after eating Indian food (curry).

Bonce – A person's head.

Bonk – To have sex with.

Bonkers – Mad, crazy.

Bonnet of a Car – The front lid of a car under which usually sits the engine; USA, the 'hood'.

Bonny (Bonnie) – Scottish for beautiful, pretty, attractive.

Bookie – Bookmaker, person or company that accepts bets.

Bookie's Runner – Person who takes another person's bets/money to the bookie.

Boom Boom – The catchphrase of puppet Basil Brush, usually used at the end of a bad joke, with a soft punch on the shoulder.

Boot of a Car – The back lid of a car, in which you usually put your suitcases, golf clubs or dead bodies.

Booze – Alcohol.

Booze Cruise – A cruise with free alcohol, or a trip to another country to buy alcohol.

Booze Hound – A heavy drinker.

Boozer – The bar, pub, licensed drinking establishment.

Bodie and Doyle - Cockney Rhyming Slang for 'oil'. (Source, UK TV show)

Boiled Beef & Carrot - Cockney Rhyming Slang for 'claret'. (blood)

Boiler House - Cockney Rhyming Slang for 'spouse'.

Bombay Duck - Cockney Rhyming Slang for 'f*ck'.

Bonnie Fair - Cockney Rhyming Slang for 'hair'.

Bonnie & Clyde - Cockney Rhyming Slang for 'snide'.

Boom & Mizzen - Cockney Rhyming Slang for 'prison'. (Source, ship's masts)

Bo Peep - Cockney Rhyming Slang for 'sleep'.

Boracic Lint – Cockney Rhyming Slang for 'skint', means broke, having no money.

Boris Becker - Cockney Rhyming Slang for 'pecker'. (Source, German tennis player)

Boris the Bold - Cockney Rhyming Slang for 'cold'.

Born & Bred - Cockney Rhyming Slang for 'dead'.

Bosie – Cuddle, hug. (Scottish)

Boss Hogg - Cockney Rhyming Slang for 'bog'. (toilet) (Source, USA TV character)

Bossyboots – A person with the attitude of being in charge, ordering other people about.

Botany Bay - Cockney Rhyming Slang for 'run away'.

Botch – To mess things up

Botched Job – A messed up job.

Bottle – Bravery, courage, bravado.

Bottle & Glass - Cockney Rhyming Slang for 'class' or 'arse'.

Bottle & Stopper - Cockney Rhyming Slang for 'copper'. (policeman)

Bottle of Beer - Cockney Rhyming Slang for 'ear', or 'queer'.

Bottle of Cola - Cockney Rhyming Slang for 'bowler'.

Bottle of Glue - Cockney Rhyming Slang for number '2'.

Bottle of Pop - Cockney Rhyming Slang for 'shop'.

Bottle of Rum - Cockney Rhyming Slang for 'bum'.

Bottle of Sauce - Cockney Rhyming Slang for 'horse'.

Bottle of Scotch - Cockney Rhyming Slang for a 'watch'.

Bottomless Pit - Cockney Rhyming Slang for 'shit'.

Boutrous Boutrous Gali - Cockney Rhyming Slang for 'charlie'. (cocaine)

Bovver – Means 'bother', or trouble.

Bow & Arrow - Cockney Rhyming Slang for 'sparrow', or 'barrow'.

Bowfin – smelly, stinking. (Scottish)

Bowl of Chalk - Cockney Rhyming Slang for 'walk'.

Bowl of Fruit - Cockney Rhyming Slang for 'suit'.

Bowler Hat - Cockney Rhyming Slang for 'twat'.

Box of Toys - Cockney Rhyming Slang for 'noise'.

Box Your Ears – Hit a person around the head.

Boyo – Welsh for male person.

Boy Racer - Young person who drives their car too fast.

Brace & Bit - Cockney Rhyming Slang for 'tit', or 'shit'.

Braces – Men's Suspenders, for holding up trousers.

Brad Pitt - Cockney Rhyming Slang for 'shit', or 'fit'.

Brad Pitts - Cockney Rhyming Slang for 'shits', or 'tits'.

Brady Bunch - Cockney Rhyming Slang for 'lunch'.

Brahms & Liszt - Cockney Rhyming Slang for 'pissed'.

Bram Stoker - Cockney Rhyming Slang for 'choker' or 'joker'.

Bram Stoking - Cockney Rhyming Slang for 'choking', or 'joking'.

Brand New – Means 'good', that you're pleased with something.

Brass Band(s) - Cockney Rhyming Slang for 'hand(s)'.

Brass Door - Cockney Rhyming Slang for 'whore'.

Brassed Off - If you are brassed off with something or someone, you are fed up. Pissed perhaps.

Brass Flute - Cockney Rhyming Slang for 'prostitute'.

Brass Monkey Weather – The weather is cold; 'freezing the balls off a Brass Monkey. (Brass Monkey was a square ring holding cannonballs in a pile on board ship. When the weather got cold, the brass shrunk, knocking the balls out.)

Brass Neck – Having over-confidence in your own actions, while not understanding that your behavior is unacceptable to others.

Brass Tacks – Basics. Getting back to Brass Tacks; getting back to the basics.

Braw – Scottish for wonderful, good, lovely, anything positive.

Bread & Butter - Cockney Rhyming Slang for 'butter', or 'nutter'.

Bread & Cheese - Cockney Rhyming Slang for 'sneeze'.

Bread & Honey - Cockney Rhyming Slang for 'money'.

Bread Knife - Cockney Rhyming Slang for 'wife'.

Break the Seal – The first toilet visit of the day or session.

Breeks – Trousers (Scottish)

Breenge – To rush in, to hurry without looking/thinking.

Brekky – Short for 'Breakfast'.

Brendan Grace - Cockney Rhyming Slang for 'face'.. (Source, Irish comedian)

Brew – A cup of tea.

Brewer's Droop – The softening effects of lots of alcohol on men's sexual performance.

Brian Clough - Cockney Rhyming Slang for 'rough', or 'puff' (gay). (Source, English football manager)

Bricks 'n' Mortar - Cockney Rhyming Slang for 'daughter'.

Bride & Groom - Cockney Rhyming Slang for 'living room'.

Bridie – Scottish pastry, filled with meat, veg.

Brigham Young - Cockney Rhyming Slang for 'tongue'.

Bright & Breezy - Cockney Rhyming Slang for 'easy'.

Brighton Pier - Cockney Rhyming Slang for 'queer'. (gay)

Brighton Sands - Cockney Rhyming Slang for 'hands'.

Brill - Short for "brilliant". Used by kids to mean cool.

Briney Marlin - Cockney Rhyming Slang for 'darlin''.

Bristols – Cockney Rhyming Slang for 'tits, a lady's breasts, 'Bristol City (soccer club) rhymes with 'titty'.

Bristol & West - Cockney Rhyming Slang for 'chest'.

Bristol City - Cockney Rhyming Slang for 'titty'.

British Summer Time – The change of an hour forward in spring for 6 months.

Britney Spears - Cockney Rhyming Slang for 'tears', 'beers', or 'ears'.

Brixton Riot - Cockney Rhyming Slang for 'diet'.

Brolly – Short for 'Umbrella'.

Bromley By Bows - Cockney Rhyming Slang for 'toes'.

Brose – Scottish oatmeal porridge.

Brown Bread – Cockney Rhyming Slang for 'dead'.

Browned Off – Angry, pissed off, or upset.

Bruce Lee - Cockney Rhyming Slang for 'key', 'tea', or 'pee'. (Source, USA Kung Fu star)

Brummie – A person from Birmingham

Brussel Sprout - Cockney Rhyming Slang for 'shout', or 'nowt', 'tout', or 'scout'.

BSE – Bovine Spongiform Encephalopathy… mad cow disease.

Bubble – To cry, weep.

Bubble and Squeak - Cockney Rhyming Slang for 'week', 'beak', or 'Greek'.

Bubble Bath - Cockney Rhyming Slang for 'laugh'. Also 2nd degree Cockney Rhyming Slang; "He's having a Bubble".

Buck – To have sex with.

Bucket & Pail - Cockney Rhyming Slang for 'jail'.

Bucketing – Raining really hard.

Bucket of Water - Cockney Rhyming Slang for 'daughter'.

Bucket & Spades - Cockney Rhyming Slang for 'AIDS'.

Budge up - If you want to sit down and someone is taking up too much space, you'd ask them to budge up - move and make some space.

Bugger - A bad or annoying person. A botched or bad job. To sodomize.

Bugger all – Nothing, zilch, zippo, zero.

Bugging – The art of annoying someone.

Bugle – Slang for 'nose'.

Bugs Bunny - Cockney Rhyming Slang for 'money'.

Builder's Bum – Visible crack of the behind between shirt and trousers.

Building Society – UK equivalent of Credit Union (rough).

Bull & Cow - Cockney Rhyming Slang for 'row'. (argument)

Bullock's Horn - Cockney Rhyming Slang for 'pawn'.

Bullseye – Slang for 50 or Fifty pounds. (centre of a dart board)

Bully Beef – Tinned corned beef, treated with salt to preserve, from the French boulii. A memory of WW2.

Bully For You – A word for praise, admirable, excellent, but usually said sarcastically.

Bum – Your ass. A tramp. To hang around doing nothing.

Bumble Bee - Cockney Rhyming Slang for 'E – Ecstacy'.

Bumfle – Scottish; a fold or runckle in clothes or carpet.

Bung - To throw, toss. "bung my car keys over, mate". A bung is also a bribe.

Bun in the Oven – Pregnant.

Bungalo – A low, one storey house.

Bunker – Scottish slang for kitchen worktop, next to sink.

Bunk Off – Play truant, be absent from, play hooky.

Bunny Ears - Cockney Rhyming Slang for 'tears'.

Bunse – Slang for 'money'. (see next entry)

Bunsen Burner - Cockney Rhyming Slang for 'earner'. (job that pays good money)

Burn – Small stream, small river. (Scottish)

Burnt Cinder - Cockney Rhyming Slang for 'window'.

Burt & Ernie - Cockney Rhyming Slang for 'journey'.

Burton on Trent - Cockney Rhyming Slang for 'rent'.

Bushel & Peck - Cockney Rhyming Slang for 'neck', or 'cheque'.

Bushey Park - Cockney Rhyming Slang for 'lark'.

Business, The – Means great, wonderful, top quality.

Busman's Holiday – A vacation (or recreation) that means you do the same thing as you do at work.

Buster Keaton - Cockney Rhyming Slang for 'meeting'.

Butchers - To have a butchers at something is to have a look. This is a cockney rhyming slang word that has become common. The reason "butchers" means a look even though it doesn't rhyme is because it is short for "butchers hook" and "hook" of course, does rhyme.

Butcher's Hook - Cockney Rhyming Slang for 'look'. Also 2nd degree Cockney Rhyming Slang; "Let me in, let's have a butcher's at it".

Butter Up – give goods, food, something good to a person to get a better response.

Butterfingers – Not holding a ball catch, a clumsy person.

Butty – Basically a sandwich. A slice of bread folded over anything. The favorite being chips; a chip butty with broon sauce.

By-Election – A single constituency election when the MP dies or resigns/is fired from his/her post.

C IS FOR CEILIDH

Cab Rank - Cockney Rhyming Slang for 'bank'.

Cabin Cruiser - Cockney Rhyming Slang for 'boozer'.

Cack – Shite, excrement, or a bad version of something.

Cack-Handed – An awkward way of doing something.

Cadbury's Snack - Cockney Rhyming Slang for 'back'.

Cadge – Borrow.

Cagoule – A waterproof jacket, stows away in a small packet. Used by hikers, campers etc.

Cain & Abel - Cockney Rhyming Slang for 'table'.

Cakehole – Mouth. "Shut yer cakehole!"

Callard & Bowsers - Cockney Rhyming Slang for 'trousers'. (Source, UK Toffee maker) Also 2nd degree Cockney Rhyming Slang; "Hold on, I'm just pulling up me Callards".

Calor Gas – A bottled gas company.

Calvin Klein - Cockney Rhyming Slang for 'wine', or 'fine'. (Source, Fashion Mogul)

Camel's Hump - Cockney Rhyming Slang for 'dump'.

Canal Boat - Cockney Rhyming Slang for 'tote'.

Canary Wharf - Cockney Rhyming Slang for 'dwarf'. (Source, Area of London)

Cancer Stick – Cigarette.

Candle Wax - Cockney Rhyming Slang for 'tax'.

Candle Wick - Cockney Rhyming Slang for 'dick'.

Canned – High, drunk, stoned.

Can I Give You a Lift? – Means; Can I give you a ride in my vehicle?

Canny – Smart, careful. (Northern)

Can of Oil - Cockney Rhyming Slang for 'boil'.

Can't Be Arsed – Means; Cannot be bothered.

Canterbury Tales - Cockney Rhyming Slang for 'Wales'.

Cape of Good Hope - Cockney Rhyming Slang for 'soap'.

Capiche? – Understand?

Capped – Means being restricted in a workplace. Also means playing football (soccer) for your country; they used to actually issue real embroidered caps (hats) to the players.

Captain Cook - Cockney Rhyming Slang for 'look', or 'book'.

Captain Kirk - Cockney Rhyming Slang for 'Turk', or 'work'.

Car & Scooter - Cockney Rhyming Slang for 'computer'.

Car Park – Means; Parking lot.

Carpet – The number '3'.

Carpet & Rugs - Cockney Rhyming Slang for 'jugs'. (breasts)

Carpet Muncher – Lesbian.

Carrier Bag – A thin polythene grocery bag, sack.

Carry On – A right mess.

Carry the Can – Be blamed for something, even something you did not do.

Carsey – Toilet, this has been changed in time to 'khazi'.

Carving Knife - Cockney Rhyming Slang for 'wife'.

Casa Blanca - Cockney Rhyming Slang for 'wanker'.

Cashier – The person who takes your money in a shop.

Casuals – A group of young men (gang) looking for a fight; usually associated with football clubs.

Casualty Ward – The Accident & Emergency department at a hospital.

Cat & Cages - Cockney Rhyming Slang for 'wages'.

Cat & Dog - Cockney Rhyming Slang for 'bog'.

Cat & Mouse - Cockney Rhyming Slang for 'house'.

Catherine Zeta Jones - Cockney Rhyming Slang for 'moans'.

Cat's Whiskers – the very best of something; the dog's bollocks.

Cattle Truck - Cockney Rhyming Slang for 'f*ck'.

Ceilidh – A traditional Scottish dance event, a barn dance. (pronounced cay-ly)

Cellar Flap - Cockney Rhyming Slang for 'tap'. (borrow)

Central Heating - Cockney Rhyming Slang for 'meeting'.

Centre Half - Cockney Rhyming Slang for 'scarf'.

Century – 100.

C'est La Vie - Cockney Rhyming Slang for 'pee'.

Chairman Mao - Cockney Rhyming Slang for 'cow'.

Chalfonts St Giles - Cockney Rhyming Slang for 'piles'. (Hemorrhoids) Also 2nd degree Cockney Rhyming Slang; "My Chalfont's are sure hurting today".

Chalk Farm - Cockney Rhyming Slang for 'arm'.

Chance Would Be A Fine Thing – No chance of something happening.

Chance Your Arm – Take a chance.

Chance Your Hand (Mitt) – Take a chance, bet.

Chancellor of the Exchequer – Man in UK Government in charge of running the country's budget, money.

Chandelier - Cockney Rhyming Slang for 'queer'.

Chap – A man, a friend. Or to knock at a door.

Chap the Door – Knocking the door.

Char – Means; Tea. Cup of char.

Charing Cross - Cockney Rhyming Slang for 'horse'. (Source, London Station)

Charing Crosser - Cockney Rhyming Slang for 'tosser'.

Charlie – Cocaine.

Charlie Bucket - Cockney Rhyming Slang for 'F*ck It'.

Charlie Chan - Cockney Rhyming Slang for 'tan'.

Charlie Chester - Cockney Rhyming Slang for 'child molester'.

Charlie Drake - Cockney Rhyming Slang for 'steak'. (Source, UK comedian)

Charlie Nash - Cockney Rhyming Slang for 'slash'. (urinate)

Charlie Pride - Cockney Rhyming Slang for 'ride'.

Charlie Ronce - Cockney Rhyming Slang for 'ponce'.

Charm & Flattery - Cockney Rhyming Slang for 'battery'.

Chas & Dave - Cockney Rhyming Slang for 'shave'. (Source, UK Singers)

Chat up - To chat someone up is to try and pick them up. If you spotted a scrummy girly in a bar you might try to chat her up. Or a girl might try and chat up a chap!

Cheap – Inexpensive, a bargain, or not well made.

Cheap at Half the Price – An expression of 'a bargain'.

Chebs – Tits, breasts. (Northern)

Cheddar Cheese - Cockney Rhyming Slang for 'keys'.

Cheeky - "Eee you cheeky monkey" was what my mother said to me all the time when I was a kid. Cheeky means you are flippant, have too much lip or are a bit of a smart arse! Generally you are considered to be a bit cheeky if you have an answer for everything and always have the last word.

Cheerful Giver - Cockney Rhyming Slang for 'liver'.

Cheerio - Not a breakfast cereal. Just a friendly way of saying goodbye. Or in the north "tara" which is pronounced sort of like "churar".

Cheers - This word is obviously used when drinking with friends. However, it also has other colloquial meanings. For example when saying goodbye you could say "cheers", or "cheers then". It also means thank you.

Cheery Bye – Good bye.

Cheese & Kisses - Cockney Rhyming Slang for 'missus'.

Cheese & Rice - Cockney Rhyming Slang for 'Jesus Christ'.

Cheesed off - This is a polite way of saying you are pissed off with something.

Cheese Rind - Cockney Rhyming Slang for 'four of a kind'.

Cheesey – Kind of corny.

Cheesey Quaver - Cockney Rhyming Slang for 'favour', or 'raver'. (Source, UK crisp snack)

Cheggers Plays Pop - Cockney Rhyming Slang for 'shop'. (Source, UK TV programme)

Chelsea Blue - Cockney Rhyming Slang for 'Jew'.

Chelsea Tractor – A 4x4 vehicle in town.

Cheltenham Bold - Cockney Rhyming Slang for 'cold'.

Chemist – A Pharmacist.

Cherie Blair - Cockney Rhyming Slang for 'Penalty Fare'. (Source, UK PM wife)

Cherry Hogg - Cockney Rhyming Slang for 'dog'.

Cherry Pie - Cockney Rhyming Slang for 'lie'.

Cherry Ripe - Cockney Rhyming Slang for 'pipe'.

Cheryl Crow - Cockney Rhyming Slang for 'snow'.

Chevy Chase - Cockney Rhyming Slang for 'face'.

Chew The Fat - Cockney Rhyming Slang for 'chat'.

Chib – Either the snib on a door lock, or to verbally pursue a matter; "She chibbed at me for ages for being late". Also to stab, a knife.

Chicken & Rice - Cockney Rhyming Slang for 'nice'.

Chicken Dinner - Cockney Rhyming Slang for 'winner'.

Chicken Dipper - Cockney Rhyming Slang for 'stripper', or 'slipper'.

Chicken Jalfrezi - Cockney Rhyming Slang for 'crazy'. (Source, Indian Curry)

Chicken Oriental - Cockney Rhyming Slang for 'mental'. (Source, Indian Curry)

Chicken Plucker - Cockney Rhyming Slang for 'f*cker'.

Chicker – Haircut.

Chief Cook and Bottle Washer – The person who knows/thinks they do every job in a specific place.

Chiel - Scottish for fellow, guy, companion.

China – An expression for Mate or Friend. Me old china. From Cockney Rhyming Slang.

China Plate - Cockney Rhyming Slang for 'mate'.

Chinese Blind - Cockney Rhyming Slang for 'mind'.

Chinese Chippy - Cockney Rhyming Slang for 'nippy'.

Ching – The number '5'.

Chinky – The local Chinese restaurant or takeaway.

Chin Wag - This is another word for a Chat. You can probably tell why!

Chinese Whispers - Refers to the way a story gets changed as is passes from one person to the next so that the end result may be completely different from what was originally said.

Chip Butty – A sandwich with potato fries on.

Chip Butty - Cockney Rhyming Slang for 'nutty'.

Chipmunks - Cockney Rhyming Slang for 'trunks'.

Chippie/Chipper – Fish & Chip Shop.

Chippy – Carpenter, joiner.

Chips – French fries.

Chips & Peas - Cockney Rhyming Slang for 'knees'.

Chitty Chitty Bang Bang - Cockney Rhyming Slang for 'Cockney Rhyming Slang'.

Chivvy along – Encourage to hurry up, hustle.

Choc Ice – A black person who speaks or acts like a white person.

Chocka – A room, venue or building which is filled to capacity.

Chocolate Frog - Cockney Rhyming Slang for 'wog'. (person of color)

Chocolate Fudge - Cockney Rhyming Slang for 'judge'.

Chop Chop – Hurry up.

CJD – Christian Jacobs Disease… the human form of BSE; mad cows disease.

Christian Ziege - Cockney Rhyming Slang for 'eager'. (Source, football star)

Christmas Crackered - Cockney Rhyming Slang for 'knackered'.

Christmas Eve - Cockney Rhyming Slang for 'believe'.

Chuck – To throw.

Chucking Out Time – Closing time, time to throw people out.

Chuddy – Chewing Gum.

Chuff – Vagina.

Chuffed – Really, really pleased. Happy, glad. You would be chuffed to bits if you were really pleased about something, grinning like a Cheshire cat, kind of pleased.

Chug – To take a big mouthful of drink.

Chugger – A beggar, a panhandler, a person who accosts people in the street for money.

C of E - The Church of England. Our official protestant church - of which the Queen is the head.

Church Pews - Cockney Rhyming Slang for 'shoes'.

Chutzpah – Courage, bravery, sometimes by trickery or gall.(pronounced hoots-pah)

Cilla Black - Cockney Rhyming Slang for 'back'. (Source, UK TV star)

Cinderella - Cockney Rhyming Slang for 'Stella Artois (beer)'.

Civvy Street – A soldiers expression for civilian life.

Claes – Clothes (Scottish).

Clair Rayners - Cockney Rhyming Slang for 'trainers'.

Clapped out – Worn out, exhausted, broken beyond repair.

Claret – Blood.

Clark Gable - Cockney Rhyming Slang for 'table'.

Clark Kent - Cockney Rhyming Slang for 'bent'.

Clarty – Really dirty.

Clear off! – Get lost! Piss off!

Clement Freuds - Cockney Rhyming Slang for 'hemorrhoids'.

Clever Clogs (Boots) – A person who is too clever, and likes to show it.

Clever Mike - Cockney Rhyming Slang for 'bike'.

Clickety Click - Cockney Rhyming Slang for '66'.

Clink – Prison.

Clippie – A person on a bus who takes/gives tickets.

Clobber – To hit someone.

Clockwork Orange – Underground trains in Glasgow, (orange coaches).

Clodhoppers – Big feet or shoes.

Clonakilty - Cockney Rhyming Slang for 'guilty'.

Cloot – Scottish for Cloth.

Clooty Dumplin' – Scottish slang for fruity cake steamed under cloth.

Close – Scottish; an alley between houses, usually roofed.

Close Your Eyes and Think of England – Lie back and accept your fate in the name of your country. Usually associated with sex.

Clot – an idiot, a clumsy person.

Cloth-Ears – A person who plays/feigns at being deaf, not hearing.

Clothes Peg - Cockney Rhyming Slang for 'egg'.

Clothes Pegs - Cockney Rhyming Slang for 'legs'.

Clout – To hit someone/something.

Clucking Bell - Cockney Rhyming Slang for 'f*cking hell'.

Cludgie – Scottish slang for bathroom, toilet.

Clunge – Vagina.

Clunk-Click – The Gov't slogan to wear seat belts.

Clype – To tell tales on, to grass. (Scottish)

Coals & Coke - Cockney Rhyming Slang for 'broke'.

Coat & Badge - Cockney Rhyming Slang for 'cadge'. (borrow)

Coat Hanger - Cockney Rhyming Slang for 'Clanger'. (mistake)

Cobblers – Rubbish. People say "what a load of cobblers".

Cobbler's Awls - Cockney Rhyming Slang for 'balls'. (testicles)

Cock & Hen - Cockney Rhyming Slang for 'ten'.

Cock a Hoop – Overjoyed, very happy

Cock and Bull Story – A pack of lies.

Cocked a Deaf 'Un – Pretended not to hear.

Cock Linnet - Cockney Rhyming Slang for 'minute'. (time)

Cock Sparrow - Cockney Rhyming Slang for 'barrow', or 'arrow'.

Cockle – Ten pounds.

Cockle & Mussells - Cockney Rhyming Slang for 'Brussells'. (sprouts)

Cockney Rhyme - Cockney Rhyming Slang for 'time'.

Cockroach - Cockney Rhyming Slang for 'coach'.

Cock up – A blunder, mess, failure to make a mistake.

Cocoa - Cockney Rhyming Slang for 'say so'.

Codswallop – Lies, wrong, untruths, falsehood.

Coffin Dodger – Old person.

Coffin Nails – Cigarettes.

Cold Chill - Cockney Rhyming Slang for 'Old Bill'. (police)

Colney Hatch - Cockney Rhyming Slang for 'match'.

Collie Buckie – Scottish slang; to carry a person on their back, legs under their arms. NOT on their shoulders.

Collywobbles – Nerves, shakes. "I can't stand snakes, they give me the collywobbles."

Colonel Gadaffi - Cockney Rhyming Slang for 'café'.

Colour Supplement – The colour magazine that accompanies many Sunday papers.

Collared - Means picked up by the police… literally by the collar.

Come a Cropper – Die, be defeated, or get injured in a surprising or terrible way.

Come Again? – Means, "Say it again", repeat yourself.

Commercial Traveler – Travelling salesman.

Commodore – 15 pounds.

Comprehensive School – Public school, co-ed.

Conan Doyle - Cockney Rhyming Slang for 'boil'.

Condoleezza Rice - Cockney Rhyming Slang for 'price'.

Conkers – Chestnuts. Kids game played for centuries, then forgotten as kids got soft.

Connaught Ranger - Cockney Rhyming Slang for 'stranger'.

Constantino Rocca - Cockney Rhyming Slang for 'shocker'. (Source, football star)

Conscription – The draft for military service.

Coochie Coo - Cockney Rhyming Slang for 'Zoo'.

Cooking Fat - Cockney Rhyming Slang for 'cat'.

Cool Beans - Good, cool, fine, okay.

Copacabana - Cockney Rhyming Slang for 'spanner'. (wrench)

Cop a Feel – Touch someone's sexy bits.

Copper – Policeman.

Cor - It will sometimes be lengthened to "cor blimey" or "cor love a duck". "Cor blimey" is a variation of "Gawd Blimey" or "Gor Blimey". All a corruption of the oath "God Blind Me".

Corbie – Scottish for crow, raven.

Corn Beef - Cockney Rhyming Slang for 'teeth'.

Corn on the Cob - Cockney Rhyming Slang for 'job'.

Corned Beef – Cockney Rhyming Slang for 'deaf'. (deef)

Cornish Pasty - Cockney Rhyming Slang for 'nasty'.

Couch Potato – A lazy person.

Council Gritter - Cockney Rhyming Slang for 'shitter'.

Counterfoil – Duplicate.

Country Cousin - Cockney Rhyming Slang for 'dozen'.

Coupon – Face. "Look at the coupon on her!"

Cousin Kyle - Cockney Rhyming Slang for 'pedophile'. (Source, South Parks)

Couthie – Scottish for friendly.

Covers – Bedlinen.

Cow – Derogatory term for a girl or lady who is free with their sexuality.

Cow & Calf - Cockney Rhyming Slang for 'half', or 'laugh'.

Cowp – Knock over.

Cowpit – Something that's knocked over or crooked.

Cozzers – Cops.

Crabbit – Scottish for irritated, angry.

Cracking - If something is cracking, it means it is the best. Usually said without pronouncing the last "G". If a girl is cracking it means she is stunning. She's a cracker!

Craic (Crack) – The chat, chatter, conversation.

Cram - Before a big exam you would be expected to cram. This simply means to study hard in the period running up to the exam.

Crap - The same word in both countries - but less rude here. I loved watching Brits being interviewed on US chat shows and embarrassing the interviewer when they said something was "total crap".

Crater Face – Someone bad with acne, or acne scars.

Cream Cookie - Cockney Rhyming Slang for 'bookie'.

Cream Crackered – Cockney Rhyming Slang for 'knackered', very tired, exhausted.

Cream Crackers - Cockney Rhyming Slang for 'knackers', testicles.

Cream Rice - Cockney Rhyming Slang for 'nice'.

Cribbage Pegs - Cockney Rhyming Slang for 'legs'.

Crikey - Another exclamation of surprise. Some people say "Crikey Moses".

Crimper – Hairdresser.

Crisps – Potato Chips.

Crispy Duck - Cockney Rhyming Slang for 'f*ck'.

Croak – Die.

Crosby Stills & Nash - Cockney Rhyming Slang for 'cash'.

Crosby Stills Nash & Young - Cockney Rhyming Slang for 'tongue'.

Crossing the Floor – Going from one party to the other in politics.

Crown Jewels - Cockney Rhyming Slang for 'tools'.

Crown Jewels – Testicles.

Crud – Dirt, mud, crap at the back of your throat, flu.

Cruising for a Bruising – (Heading for a spreading) To be heading for a battle, fight, probably not going to turn out well.

Crumpet – Someone nice of the opposite sex.

Crust of Bread - Cockney Rhyming Slang for 'head'.

Crusty Dragon - A nose booger; one of the really crispy ones.

Cuddle & Kiss - Cockney Rhyming Slang for 'miss'.

Cuff Link - Cockney Rhyming Slang for 'drink'.

Cullen Skink – Scottish soup, made from smoked haddock.

C*nt Flap - Cockney Rhyming Slang for 'slap'.

Cupid's Dart - Cockney Rhyming Slang for 'fart'.

Cupid Stunt – Spoonerism. Stupid C*nt.

Currant Bun - Cockney Rhyming Slang for 'fun', 'son', or 'nun'.

Currant Cakey - Cockney Rhyming Slang for 'shaky'.

Cushty – Good, fine, right.

Custard & Jelly - Cockney Rhyming Slang for 'telly'. (TV)

Cut of Your Jib – The way you look, your style.

Cutlery – Silverware to eat with.

Cuts & Scratches - Cockney Rhyming Slang for 'matches'.

Cutty Sark - Cockney Rhyming Slang for 'loan shark'.

CV - Curriculum Vitae (resumé)

Cynthia Payne - Cockney Rhyming Slang for 'rain'.

D IS FOR DOG'S BOLLOCKS

Dab Hand – Good at something, expert, skillful.

Daddy Longlegs - Long legged flying insect.

Dad's Army - Cockney Rhyming Slang for 'barmy'. (Source, UK TV Show)

Daffadown Dilly - Cockney Rhyming Slang for 'silly'.

Daffy Duck - Cockney Rhyming Slang for 'f*ck'.

Daft – Silly, idiot, not clever.

Daft & Barmy - Cockney Rhyming Slang for 'army'.

Daft a'path - Short for a daft half penny (in old money). Stupid, daft.

Dago – Of Spanish, Italian or Portuguese descent.

Daily Mail - Cockney Rhyming Slang for 'tale'. (Source, UK Newspaper)

Dairylea - Cockney Rhyming Slang for 'wee'. (pee) (Source, UK Processed Cheese)

Daisy Roots - Cockney Rhyming Slang for 'boots'.

Damage – Cost. "I want that shirt. What's the damage?"

Dame Edna Everidge - Cockney Rhyming Slang for 'beverage'. (Source, Aus star)

Dame Judy Dench - Cockney Rhyming Slang for 'stench'. (Source, UK Actress)

Damien Duff - Cockney Rhyming Slang for 'rough'.

Damien Hirst - Cockney Rhyming Slang for 'degree'. (University honor)

Dancing Bears - Cockney Rhyming Slang for 'stairs'.

Dancing Fleas - Cockney Rhyming Slang for 'keys'.

Dander – A short look at something.

Dangermouse - Cockney Rhyming Slang for 'spouse'.

Dangly Bits – A man's sex bits.

Daniel Boone - Cockney Rhyming Slang for 'spoon'.

Daniel Fergus McGrain - Cockney Rhyming Slang for 'train'.

Danny Glover - Cockney Rhyming Slang for 'lover'.

Danny La Rue - Cockney Rhyming Slang for 'clue'. (Source, UK Star)

Danny Marr - Cockney Rhyming Slang for 'car'.

Darius Rucker - Cockney Rhyming Slang for 'f*cker'.

Darky Cox - Cockney Rhyming Slang for 'box'.

Darren Day - Cockney Rhyming Slang for 'gay'.

Darren Gough - Cockney Rhyming Slang for 'cough'.

Davey Crocket - Cockney Rhyming Slang for 'pocket'.

David Batty - Cockney Rhyming Slang for 'tatty'.

David Blaine - Cockney Rhyming Slang for 'insane'.

David Boon - Cockney Rhyming Slang for 'spoon'.

David Gower - Cockney Rhyming Slang for 'shower'. (Source, cricketer)

David Hockney - Cockney Rhyming Slang for 'cockney'.

David Jason - Cockney Rhyming Slang for 'mason'. (Source, UK Actor)

David Mellor - Cockney Rhyming Slang for 'Stella (beer)'. (Source, UK politician)

David Starkey - Cockney Rhyming Slang for 'parky'. (cold) (Source, TV historian)

Davina McCalls - Cockney Rhyming Slang for 'balls'.

Dawn French - Cockney Rhyming Slang for 'stench'. (Source, UK actress)

Dawson's Creek - Cockney Rhyming Slang for 'streak'.

Day Trippers - Cockney Rhyming Slang for 'slippers'.

Day's Dawning - Cockney Rhyming Slang for 'morning'.

Day's Work - 100

Dead Cert – A sure thing.

Dead Horse - Cockney Rhyming Slang for 'sauce'.

Dead Loss - Cockney Rhyming Slang for 'boss'.

Dead Meat – An obvious victim, someone certain to get set upon, beat up.

Dear Ringer - Cockney Rhyming Slang for 'minger'. (smelly)

Dear – Expensive, costing too much.

Debag – To pull someone's trousers off.

Deaf & Dumb - Cockney Rhyming Slang for 'bum'.

Deep Fat Fryer - Cockney Rhyming Slang for 'liar'.

Deep Sea Diver - Cockney Rhyming Slang for 'fiver'. (5 pounds)

Deep Sea Glider - Cockney Rhyming Slang for 'cider'.

Dekko - To have a quick look at something.

De La Soul - Cockney Rhyming Slang for 'dole'.

Delhi Belli – An upset stomach after Indian food, curry.

Demerara Sugar – Brown sugar.

Dennis & Gnasher - Cockney Rhyming Slang for 'badger'.

Dental Flosser - Cockney Rhyming Slang for 'tosser'.

Derby Kelly - Cockney Rhyming Slang for 'belly'.

Derek Randall - Cockney Rhyming Slang for 'love handle(s)'.

Desmond Hacket - Cockney Rhyming Slang for 'jacket'.

Desmond Tutu - Cockney Rhyming Slang for '2nd class honors (university)'. (Source, politician)

Desperate Dans - Cockney Rhyming Slang for 'cans'. (headphones) (Source, comic character)

Dialing Code – Dialing tone in old phones.

Diamond Rocks - Cockney Rhyming Slang for 'socks'.

Dibs & Dabs - Cockney Rhyming Slang for 'crabs'.

Dicksplash – An idiot, a stupid person.

Dick Van Dyke - Cockney Rhyming Slang for 'bike'.

Dicky – If talking about health, it's not good. To have a dicky tummy, means feeling unwell. Also means unstable, rocky, perhaps not made well. "he's standing on that pile of stones, but it looks pretty dicky to me".

Dicky Bird – Cockney Rhyming Slang for 'word'.

Dickie Bird - Cockney Rhyming Slang for '3rd class honors'. (university) (Source, cricket ref)

Dickory Dock - Cockney Rhyming Slang for 'clock'.

Dicky Dirt - Cockney Rhyming Slang for 'shirt'.

Diddle - To rip someone off or to con someone is to diddle them. When you go overseas, check your change to make sure you haven't been diddled!

Diddly Squat – Nothing, zero.

Didgeridoo - Cockney Rhyming Slang for 'screw'. (prison officer)

Digestive Biscuits – Crumbly sugar cookies.

Digital Detox – A period away from technology, internet, etc.

Digs – the place where you stay, usually rented or holiday.

Dilly Dally – To waste time, to fudge around.

Dim/Dimbo - A dim person is stupid or thick or a dimwit. Dimwit - Someone a bit on the dim side.

Din-Dins – Dinner.

Ding Dong - Cockney Rhyming Slang for 'song', or 'bong'.

Ding Dong Bell - Cockney Rhyming Slang for 'hell'.

Dinner Plate - Cockney Rhyming Slang for 'mate'.

Dipstick – An idiot.

Dirty Beast - Cockney Rhyming Slang for 'priest'.

Dirty Den - Cockney Rhyming Slang for 'ten' or 110 pounds.

Dirty Stopout – Staying away from home all night having sex.

Dirty Weekend – A weekend away from home having sex.

Dish/Dishy - If someone is a bit of a dish or a bit dishy it means they are attractive or good looking.

Dispatch Rider – Motorcycle messenger.

Divorced His Ankles and Married His Knees – Trousers too short.

Divvy – Stupid. Also to divide. "Divvy the spoils".

Dixie Deans - Cockney Rhyming Slang for 'jeans'. (Source, footballer)

DIY - This is short for "do it yourself" and applies not just to the DIY stores but also to anything that you need to do yourself. For example, if we get really bad service in a restaurant (oh, you noticed!) then we might ask the waiter if it is a DIY restaurant - just to wind them up.

Do - A posh party. You would go to a "do" if you were going to a party in the UK. The Queen has "do's" all the time.

Do - If you go into a shop and say "do you do batteries?" it means "do you sell batteries".

Do – Prosecute; If you drive along a motorway in the wrong lane the police will 'do' you. You could then tell your friends that you have been 'done' by the police.

Do a Bunk – Up and leave house/home (usually in the middle of the night) to avoid rent or other consequences.

Do a Runner – To run away, usually to avoid consequences.

Do As You Likey - Cockney Rhyming Slang for 'pikey'.

Dobber - A stupid person, a tell-tale.

Doctor Crippen - Cockney Rhyming Slang for 'bread & dripping'.

Dodge & Swerve - Cockney Rhyming Slang for 'perve'.

Do me Goods - Cockney Rhyming Slang for 'woods'.

Do your Nut – Go crazy.

Doddle - Something that is a doddle, is a cinch, it's easy.

Dodgy - If someone or something is a bit dodgy, it is not to be trusted. Dodgy food should be thrown away at home, or sent back in a restaurant. Dodgy people are best avoided. You never know what they are up to. Dodgy goods may have been nicked (stolen). A town may have certain areas which are a bit dodgy and should be avoided!

Does What it Says on the Tin – Something that acts exactly as it should.

Dog – Ugly girl or woman.

Dog & Bone - Cockney Rhyming Slang for 'phone'.

Dog & Lead - Cockney Rhyming Slang for 'weed'.

Dog's Eye – Cockney Rhyming Slang for 'meat pie'.

Dog's Knob - Cockney Rhyming Slang for 'job'.

Dogging – Having sex with a stranger in public.

Dog's Bollocks - You would say that something really fantastic was the dog's bollocks. Comes from the fact that a dog's bollocks are so fantastic that he can't stop licking them! Nice huh? Often shortened to just "The dog's".

Dog's Dinner (or Dog's Breakfast) - If you make a real mess of something it might be described as a real dog's dinner.

Doing a Ton – Driving over 100mph.

Doing the Washing Up – Washing the dishes.

Doll – Girl, woman.

Dolly Mixtures - Cockney Rhyming Slang for 'pictures'. (cinema)

Dome Good - Cockney Rhyming Slang for 'wood'.

Dominie – Scottish for schoolmaster.

Donald Duck - Cockney Rhyming Slang for 'luck', or 'f*ck'.

Donald Ducking - Cockney Rhyming Slang for 'clucking'. (craving more heroin)

Donald Trump - Cockney Rhyming Slang for 'dump', or 'hump'.

Doner Kebab - Cockney Rhyming Slang for 'stab'.

Doner Kebab – Usually lamb in the form of an elephant's leg, grilled, and put in a pita bread with veggies and spicy sauce. This has nothing to do with the Doner party that committed cannibalism in USA...

Donkey Kong - Cockney Rhyming Slang for 'long'.

Donkeys Ears - Cockney Rhyming Slang for 'years'.

Donnie Darko - Cockney Rhyming Slang for 'sparko'. (asleep)

Don Revie - Cockney Rhyming Slang for 'bevvy'. (Source, footballer)

Don't Get Your knickers In a Twist – Don't get upset about something.

Don't Give a Monkey's – Don't give a damn about something, oblivious.

Don't Teach Your Grandmother To Suck Eggs – Don't teach an older person what to do, when they already know.

Done Over – Beaten, assaulted.

Done Up Like a Kipper – Beaten really hard.

Donkeys Years - Someone said to me the other day that they hadn't seen me for donkey's years. It means they hadn't seen me for ages.

Doo – A pigeon.

Doogie Howsers - Cockney Rhyming Slang for 'trousers'.

Dook or Dooking for Apples – Scottish Halloween game, fishing for apples in a large basin of water (using only your teeth).

Doolalley – Crazy. "Don't ask her, she's doolalley."

Doon – Down (Scottish)

Doric – Dialect spoken in the north east of Scotland.

Doris Day - Cockney Rhyming Slang for 'gay'.

Dosh - Money, cash.

Dosser – Homeless person.

Dot & Dash - Cockney Rhyming Slang for 'cash'.

Dot Cotton - Cockney Rhyming Slang for 'rotten'.

Double Dutch - Cockney Rhyming Slang for 'crutch'.

Dough – Money, cash.

Doug McClure - Cockney Rhyming Slang for 'whore'.

Douglas Hurd - Cockney Rhyming Slang for 'turd', (shit) or 3rd class honors (university)

Down in the Dumps – Feeling depressed, underwhelmed, a bit down.

Down The Drains - Cockney Rhyming Slang for 'brains'.

Down the Swanie – Lost, gone, same as 'up the swanie'.

Down the Tubes – Lost, gone.

Dram – Scottish small drink of whisky.

Draughts – The game of Checkers.

Drawing Pin – Thumb-tack.

Dreaded Lurgy – Sickness, illness. A bad case of influenza.

Dreep – Scottish for drip, also for letting oneself down a wall by hanging on, then falling.

Dreich – Scottish for wet, miserable weather, not quite fully raining.

Dressing Table – Drawer unit with mirror in a bedroom.

Dribbling – Running with the football (soccer ball) at your feet.

Drookit – Really soaking wet. (Scottish)

Drooth – Very thirsty. (Scottish)

Drop a Clanger – To make a mistake, to misinterpret a situation, to put your foot in it.

Drop the Kids off at the Pool – Shite, defecate.

Drop Your Guts – Fart.

Drop You Right in It – Drop you in the deep end.

Dross - Bad, very bad, rubbish, also small change.

Drouthy – Scottish for thirsty, usually the morning after.

Drum – Your house, home, where you lay your head.

Drum & Bass - Cockney Rhyming Slang for 'face', or 'place'.

Drum & Fife - Cockney Rhyming Slang for 'knife'.

Drum Roll - Cockney Rhyming Slang for 'hole'.

Duane Eddies - Cockney Rhyming Slang for 'readies'. (cash)

Duchess of Fife - Cockney Rhyming Slang for 'wife'.

Duck/Ducks – A term of endearment.

Duck and Dive - Cockney Rhyming Slang for 'skive'.

Ducks Arse - Cockney Rhyming Slang for 'grass'.

Ducking and Diving – Weaving through life

Dud – Not working, broken.

Dudley Moore - Cockney Rhyming Slang for 'score'. (20 pounds)

Dudley Moore's - Cockney Rhyming Slang for 'sores'.

Duff – a bad shot at a sport. Golf, swinging but hitting the ball badly; a duff shot, or a duffer. Also, not working, also a woman's front sex part. Also "Up the Duff" means you're pregnant.

Duffer - Any person that is duff could be referred to as a duffer. A bad shot at golf.

Duke & Daisy – Cockney Rhyming Slang for 'Chicken Jahlfrezi', a type of Indian Curry.

Duke of Argyles - Cockney Rhyming Slang for 'piles'. (Hemorrhoids)

Duke of Kent - Cockney Rhyming Slang for 'rent', or 'bent'.

Duke of Montrose - Cockney Rhyming Slang for 'nose'.

Duke of Spain - Cockney Rhyming Slang for 'rain'.

Duke of York - Cockney Rhyming Slang for 'cork', 'chalk', or 'fork'.

Dull - No longer sharp.

Dump – A shite, to shite, a defecation.

Dundonian – Scottish, a person from Dundee.

Dunkirk Spirit – Never say die spirit, Indefatigability, Strength under pressure.

Dunlop Tyre - Cockney Rhyming Slang for 'liar'.

Dunny – Toilet, from Australia.

Dustbin – Trashcan.

Dustbin Lid - Cockney Rhyming Slang for 'kid'.

Dustman – Trashman.

Dusty Bin - Cockney Rhyming Slang for 'chin'.

Duvet – Coverlet for a bed, European in design.

Dwight Yorke - Cockney Rhyming Slang for 'pork'. (Source, footballer)

E IS FOR EDGAR ALLEN POES

Early Doors – Early in time, premature.

Early Doors - Cockney Rhyming Slang for 'drawers'. (knickers)

Early Hour(s) - Cockney Rhyming Slang for 'flower(s)'.

Eartha Kitt - Cockney Rhyming Slang for 'shit'.

Eartha Kitts - Cockney Rhyming Slang for 'tits'.

Earwig - Cockney Rhyming Slang for 'twig'. (understand)

Earwig – Listen in to, overhear.

Easter Bunny - Cockney Rhyming Slang for 'funny'.

Easy Peasy – (lemon squeasy) A childish term for something very easy. You might say it's a snap.

Easy Rider - Cockney Rhyming Slang for 'cider'.

Eddie Grundies - Cockney Rhyming Slang for 'undies'. (underwear)

Eddy Grant - Cockney Rhyming Slang for 'plant'.

Edgar Allen Poes - Cockney Rhyming Slang for 'toes'.

Edna Everage - Cockney Rhyming Slang for 'beverage'.

Eegit/Eejit – A numpty, an idiot, stupid person.

Efan Ekuku - Cockney Rhyming Slang for 'poo poo'.

Effing and Blinding – Swearing a lot.

Egg – Person.

Egg & Spoon - Cockney Rhyming Slang for 'coon', (black person)

Egghead – A boffin, clever guy, academic expert.

Eggs & Kippers - Cockney Rhyming Slang for 'slippers'.

Eh Up Duck – How are you?

Eiffel Tower - Cockney Rhyming Slang for 'shower'.

Eighteen Pence - Cockney Rhyming Slang for 'sense'.

Elastic Bands - Cockney Rhyming Slang for 'hands'.

Elbow Grease – Big effort, hard work.

Electric Soup – Scottish for whisky.

Elephant & Castle - Cockney Rhyming Slang for 'arsehole'. (Source, London suburb)

Elephants Trunk - Cockney Rhyming Slang for 'drunk'.

El Vino Collapso – Cheap wine to make you drunk quickly.

Elevenses – Meal at eleven am. Between breakfast and lunch.

Elizabeth Regina - Cockney Rhyming Slang for 'vagina'.

Elliot Ness - Cockney Rhyming Slang for 'mess'.

Elmer Fudd - Cockney Rhyming Slang for 'spud'. (potato)

Elsie Tanner - Cockney Rhyming Slang for 'spanner'. (wrench)

Elvis – 3rd degree Cockney Rhyming Slang for 'hair'. From Aaron-'hair-on'. "Calm down, mate, keep your Elvis.

Emma Freuds - Cockney Rhyming Slang for 'hemorrhoids'.

Empire State - Cockney Rhyming Slang for 'mate'.

Engaged – A busy signal on the phone.

Engineers & Stokers - Cockney Rhyming Slang for 'brokers'.

English Lit - Cockney Rhyming Slang for 'shit'.

Ernie Marsh - Cockney Rhyming Slang for 'grass'.

Errol Flynn - Cockney Rhyming Slang for 'chin'.

Essex Girl – Low class girl or woman

Estate Agent – Realtor.

Ethan Hunt - Cockney Rhyming Slang for 'c*nt'.

Euan Blair - Cockney Rhyming Slang for 'Leicester Square'.

Ewan McGregor - Cockney Rhyming Slang for 'beggar'.

Exactly what it Says on the Tin – Means 'something does what it says it will', from a Ronseal varnish commercial.

Excuse me – An exclamation of sorry, used after farting or belching in public.

Ex-Directory – A Phone number not in the common directory, hidden.

Ex-Serviceman – A veteran.

Extracting the Urine – Literally 'taking the piss', making fun of.

Eyeball – To have a close look at something, to have an "eyeball".

Eye Lash - Cockney Rhyming Slang for 'slash'. (urinate)

Eyes Front - Cockney Rhyming Slang for 'c*nt'.

Eyetie – Someone from Italy.

F IS FOR FLASH HARRY

F. Off. – F*ck off.

Face Ache - Derogatory term for an annoying person.

Face Like a Bag of Hammers/Chisels – Really ugly.

Face Like a Smacked Arse – A sour look, expression.

Face like a Smacked Toad - Ugly

Face Like Fizz – Really angry and holding it back.

Face Fungus – Facial hair of any kind.

Faff Around – Dither, waste time, fanny around.

Fag – Cigarette, also homosexual.

Fag Ash Lil – Woman who smokes a lot.

Fagged - If you are too lazy or tired to do something you could say "I can't be fagged". It means you can't be Bothered.

Fagging - Fagging is the practice of making new boys at boarding schools into slaves for the older boys. If you are fagging for an older boy you might find yourself running his bath, cleaning his shoes or performing more undesirable tasks.

Fag Hag – A woman who has friendships with gay men.

Fair Cop – A fair assessment or arrest.

Fair Crack of the Whip – A fair chance.

Fair to Middling – Medium grade, just generally middle. "How you doing, Spike? Oh, fair to middling."

Faith & Hope - Cockney Rhyming Slang for 'soap'.

Fakey Ned - Cockney Rhyming Slang for 'bed'.

False Start - Cockney Rhyming Slang for 'fart'.

Family Jewels – Testicles.

Fancy – To desire something, either people or food.

Fancy the Pants Off – To like someone sexually.

Fankle - Scottish for tangle.

Fandabidozi – Great, superb, good.

Fanny – Vagina.

Fanny around – Mucking about, wasting time, procrastination.

Fanny Craddock - Cockney Rhyming Slang for 'haddock'. (Source, TV chef)

Fanny Pad – Woman's hygiene towel.

Fanny Magnet – A good looking guy/object that attracts women.

Fantabulosa – Fantastic, great, wonderful, good.

Far East - Cockney Rhyming Slang for 'priest'.

Farmers Daughter - Cockney Rhyming Slang for 'quarter'.

Farmer Jiles - Cockney Rhyming Slang for 'piles'.

Farmers Pig - Cockney Rhyming Slang for 'wig'.

Farmers Truck - Cockney Rhyming Slang for 'f*ck'.

Fat Boy Slim - Cockney Rhyming Slang for 'gym'.

Father Ted - Cockney Rhyming Slang for 'dead'.

Fawlty Tower - Cockney Rhyming Slang for 'shower'.

Feather & Flip - Cockney Rhyming Slang for 'kip'. (sleep)

Feathers – 33.

Feck! – A substitute for 'f*ck'.

Fell Off the Back of a Lorry – Illegally obtained, stolen.

Fellow-Me-Lad – Young man, or boy.

Fergal Sharkey - Cockney Rhyming Slang for 'darkie', or 'car keys'.

Ferret & Stoat - Cockney Rhyming Slang for 'throat'.

Ferret Out – Investigate.

Fess Up – Confess, own up.

Field of Wheat - Cockney Rhyming Slang for 'street'.

Fiddle Sticks – alternative for the f-word.

Fife & Drum - Cockney Rhyming Slang for 'bum'.

Filch - To filch is to steal or pilfer.

Fill Your Boots – To eat/drink your fill.

Filling Station – Gas station.

Filly – A girl, woman.

Filter Tips - Cockney Rhyming Slang for 'lips'.

Filth – Police.

Filthy Lucre – Stolen money or goods.

Fine & Dandy - Cockney Rhyming Slang for 'brandy'.

Finger & Thumb - Cockney Rhyming Slang for 'mum', or 'rum'.

Finsbury Park - Cockney Rhyming Slang for 'mark'.

Firemans Hose - Cockney Rhyming Slang for 'nose'.

First Dibs – First choice.

First Foot – Scottish for first visitor after the new year.

Fish & Chips - Cockney Rhyming Slang for 'hips'.

Fish Hook - Cockney Rhyming Slang for 'book'.

Fish 'n' Taters - Cockney Rhyming Slang for 'laters'.

Fishermans Daughter - Cockney Rhyming Slang for 'water'.

Fishing Rod - Cockney Rhyming Slang for 'PC Plod'. (policeman)

Fit – Good-looking, tasty! A toned body.

Fit For the Knacker's Yard – Ready to die,

Fit-Up – Falsely accuse, to falsely convict, to set up.

Five to Four - Cockney Rhyming Slang for 'sure'.

Five to Two - Cockney Rhyming Slang for 'Jew'.

Fizzog – Face.

Fizzy Drink - Cockney Rhyming Slang for 'chink'.

Flag – Flat paving stone.

Flaming Nora – Exclamation of surprise or shock.

Flange – To have sex with. (Scottish)

Flash Harry – A (too) well-dressed man.

Fleas & Itches - Cockney Rhyming Slang for 'pictures'.

Fleece – To steal from.

Fleetwood Mac - Cockney Rhyming Slang for 'back'.

Flight Lieutenant Biggles - Cockney Rhyming Slang for 'giggles'.

Flipping - An alternative to the curse word 'bloody'. You'll hear people say "flipping hell" or "not flipping likely" for example.

Flit – To move house.

Flog - To sell.

Flounder & Dab - Cockney Rhyming Slang for 'cab'.

Flowers & Frolics - Cockney Rhyming Slang for 'bollocks'.

Flowery Dell - Cockney Rhyming Slang for 'cell'.

Fluffy Bunny - Cockney Rhyming Slang for 'money'.

Fluke - By chance, lucky.

Flutter - To have a bet.

Fly a Kite - Cockney Rhyming Slang for 'shite'.

Fly By Nights - Cockney Rhyming Slang for 'tights'.

Flying F*ck - Nothing. Much more than just saying 'f*ck'.

Flying Low – Having your flies undone.

Flying Without a License - Having your flies undone.

Flyover - Arial roadway.

Foot Pump - Cockney Rhyming Slang for 'dump'.

Fore & Aft - Cockney Rhyming Slang for 'daft'.

Forest Gump - Cockney Rhyming Slang for 'dump'. (shit)

Forsythe Saga - Cockney Rhyming Slang for 'lager'.

Fortnight - Two weeks. Comes from an abbreviation of "fourteen nights". Hence terms like "I'm off for a fortnights holiday" meaning "I am going on a two week vacation".

Forty Four - Cockney Rhyming Slang for 'whore'.

Forty Winks – A short snooze.

Four by Two - Cockney Rhyming Slang for 'Jew', or 'poo'.

Four Eyes – Wearing glasses.

Four Minute Miles - Cockney Rhyming Slang for 'piles'. (hemorrhoids)

Four Seasons - Cockney Rhyming Slang for 'reasons'.

Fouter – Scottish for fiddle with, mess about with.

Frank & Pat - Cockney Rhyming Slang for 'chat'.

Frank Bough - Cockney Rhyming Slang for 'off'.

Frank Skinner - Cockney Rhyming Slang for 'dinner'.

Frankie DeTory - Cockney Rhyming Slang for 'story'.

Frankie Howard - Cockney Rhyming Slang for 'coward'.

Franky Vaughn - Cockney Rhyming Slang for 'porn'.

Franz Klammer - Cockney Rhyming Slang for 'hammer'.

Frasier Crane - Cockney Rhyming Slang for 'pain'.

Frazer Nash - Cockney Rhyming Slang for 'slash'. (urinate)

Fred Astaire - Cockney Rhyming Slang for 'hair', or 'chair'.

Fred McMurry - Cockney Rhyming Slang for 'curry'.

Fred McMurrays - Cockney Rhyming Slang for 'worries'.

French Letter – A contraceptive.

French Plait - Cockney Rhyming Slang for 'flat'.

Friar Tuck - Cockney Rhyming Slang for 'f*ck', or 'luck'.

Fridge Freezer - Cockney Rhyming Slang for 'geezer'.

Frog – A French person.

Frog and Toad - Cockney Rhyming Slang for 'road'.

Fromage Frais - Cockney Rhyming Slang for 'gay'.

Front Bottom – Front sexual parts.

Front Wheel Skid - Cockney Rhyming Slang for 'Yid'. (Jew)

Fruit Gum - Cockney Rhyming Slang for 'chum'.

Fruit & Nuts - Cockney Rhyming Slang for 'guts'.

Fruity - Feeling frisky.

Fry-Up – A meal of fried stuff, usually breakfast or dinner.

Fud – A complete fool. Also vagina.

Fugly – Short for 'F*cking Ugly', really ugly.

Full Monty – The full amount, also to strip completely.

Full of Beans - To have loads of energy.

Full Shilling – Be all there, 100%.

Full Stop – Period.

Fun Bags – Breasts.

Funfair – Carnival.

Funk Soul Brother - Cockney Rhyming Slang for 'lover'.

Fur Rugs - Cockney Rhyming Slang for 'drugs'.

Furry Boots - Cockney Rhyming Slang for 'where abouts?'.

Furry Muff - Cockney Rhyming Slang for 'fair enough'.

Fuss-Pot – a person who is too fussy, too fastidious.

Fuzzy Duck - Cockney Rhyming Slang for 'f*ck'.

G IS FOR GET STUFFED

Gabbing – Gossiping, talking, usually without substance.

Gaff – House or home.

Gaffer - Boss, foreman, person in charge.

Gagging for It – Desperate for something, can be a pint, but usually sex.

Gallus – Scottish for daring, with a swagger.

Gallivanting - The dictionary says "to gad about", which probably doesn't help much! It means fooling around or horseplay. Also holidaying, or taking time off, going places.

Gam – A blowjob.

Game of Two Halves – football cliché, each half was different.

Game On – Describes something starting, the beginning.

Gamma Ray - Cockney Rhyming Slang for 'stray'.

Gammy – Something that does not work right, handicapped.

Gander - To look around.

Gandhi's Revenge – Upset stomach after having Indian food, curry.

Gang & Mob - Cockney Rhyming Slang for 'gob'. (mouth)

Ganja – Marijuana.

Garden Fence - Cockney Rhyming Slang for 'dense'.

Garden Gate - Cockney Rhyming Slang for '8th of coke', magistrate', or 'mate'.

Garden Hose - Cockney Rhyming Slang for 'nose'.

Garden Tool - Cockney Rhyming Slang for 'fool'.

Gareth Gates - Cockney Rhyming Slang for 'mates'.

Gareth Hunt - Cockney Rhyming Slang for 'c*nt'.

Garry Abblett - Cockney Rhyming Slang for 'tablet'.

Gary Glitter - Cockney Rhyming Slang for 'bitter beer', or 'shitter', or 'squitters'.

Gary Neville - Cockney Rhyming Slang for 'level'. (Source, footballer)

Gary Player - Cockney Rhyming Slang for 'all-dayer'. (drinking session) (Source, golfer)

Gash – Vagina. Also dismal.

Gasping – To really want something.

Gates of Rome - Cockney Rhyming Slang for 'home'.

Gawd Blimey – Exclamation of shock, surprise.

Gawds Truth - Cockney Rhyming Slang for 'roof'.

Gawp – Stare at.

Gay – Weak or iffeminate.

Gay & Frisky - Cockney Rhyming Slang for 'whiskey'.

Gay-Dar – A so-called sense by which homosexuals can spot other homosexuals.

Gazumped – Beaten by someone else's bid, usually in house buying.

GBH – Grievous Bodily Harm.

GBH of the Earhole – Someone talking at you too much.

GCHQ – Government Communications Headquarters.

GCSE – English lower high school qualifications.

Gear – Tools, sports paraphernalia stuff for the job.

Geez – Give. Short for 'give us'.

Geezer – Man.

Geggy – Mouth (Glasgow)

Gen - Gen means information. If you have the gen then you know what is going on.

Gender Bender – A person who defies their own gender in the way they act or dress.

Gen up - To research a subject or to get some information.

Geoff Hoon - Cockney Rhyming Slang for 'babboon'.

Geoff Hurst - Cockney Rhyming Slang for 'first class degree', or 'thirst', or 'burst'. (Source, footballer)

George & Zippy - Cockney Rhyming Slang for 'nippy'. (cold) (Source, TV puppets)

George Best - Cockney Rhyming Slang for 'chest'. (Source, footballer)

George Bush - Cockney Rhyming Slang for 'mush'. (face)

George Cole - Cockney Rhyming Slang for 'dole'. (Source, actor)

George Michael - Cockney Rhyming Slang for 'cycle', or 'menstrual cycle'.

George Raft - Cockney Rhyming Slang for 'draught'.

Georgie Bests - Cockney Rhyming Slang for 'breasts'.

Georgio Armani - Cockney Rhyming Slang for 'sarnie'. (sandwich)

German Band - Cockney Rhyming Slang for 'hand'.

German Beer - Cockney Rhyming Slang for 'engineer'.

German Cruiser - Cockney Rhyming Slang for 'boozer'. (pub)

German Fighter - Cockney Rhyming Slang for 'lighter'.

Gerry Rigged – For some reason, this means half-done, or just put together by duck tape. (Oblivious to the fact that the Germans have a superb record for doing stuff). Same as Nigger-rigged in the USA.

Gert & Daisy - Cockney Rhyming Slang for 'crazy'.

Gertie Gitana - Cockney Rhyming Slang for 'banana'.

Get Knotted – Get lost, go away.

Get Lost! - Politely translated as go away, this is really a mild way of telling someone to f*** off!

Get Off – Hook up.

Get On My Wick – To annoy, get on ones nerves.

Get On My Tits - To annoy, get on ones nerves.

Get Some In – To put in service. To put time in a project/job.

Get Stuffed! - Get lost, go away.

Get That Down Your Neck – Drink/eat that!

Getting off - This seems to be the objective of most teenagers on a big night out. Getting off with someone means making out or snogging them.

Get Weaving – To start something, to get going, to leave.

Get Your Knickers in a Twist – Get annoyed, angry.

Get Your Leg Over – Have sex.

Get Your P45 – be fired, sacked, made redundant.

Gianluca Vialli - Cockney Rhyming Slang for 'charlie'. (Source, footballer)

Giggle & Titter - Cockney Rhyming Slang for 'bitter beer'.

Gilly Mint - Cockney Rhyming Slang for 'bint'.

Ginger – A red-haired person.

Ginger Ale - Cockney Rhyming Slang for 'jail'.

Ginger Beer - Cockney Rhyming Slang for 'engineer', or 'queer'.

Ginnel – Alleyway between houses, usually roofed, vennel, close.

Ginormous – very big… bigger than enormous.

Giraffe - Cockney Rhyming Slang for 'laugh'.

Girl Crush – An attraction between two girls.

Git – A very generic insult.

Give Over – Stop it, stop talking.

Give Us a Bell - This simply means call me on the phone. In the UK, you often hear people use the word "us" to mean "me".

Glaikit – Pronounced glay-kit. Scottish for looking stupid, appearing silly.

Glasgow Kiss – Scottish; a heatbutt.

Glasgow Rangers - Cockney Rhyming Slang for 'strangers'.

Glasshouse – Greenhouse.

Glassing – An attack with a broken glass or bottle.

Glass of Water - Cockney Rhyming Slang for 'quarter'.

Glaswegian – Scottish for someone from Glasgow, also a 'weidgie'.

Glen Campbell - Cockney Rhyming Slang for 'gamble'.

Glenn Hoddle - Cockney Rhyming Slang for 'doddle'. (easy) (Source, footballer)

Gloaming – Scottish for evening, sunset, dusk.

Gloop – Sticky, gooey liquid, mud.

Gloria Gaynors - Cockney Rhyming Slang for 'trainers'.

Glossies – The colour magazines.

Glove Box – the small cupboard in front of a passenger in a car.

Go Ape – Go crazy.

Gob - Your mouth. Also to spit.

Gobshite – Irish expression for an unpopular, irritating person.

Gobsmacked – So flabbergasted, you have nothing to say.

Gobstopper – Large gumball.

Go Commando – Go without underwear.

God Botherer – A zealous religious person.

God Forbid - Cockney Rhyming Slang for 'kid'.

Godforsaken - Cockney Rhyming Slang for 'bacon'.

Go Down a Bomb – Fail absolutely. Get no applause.

God's Glory - Cockney Rhyming Slang for 'gory'.

Goggles – Glasses, spectacles.

Going 90 to the Dozen – Going really fast.

Going to See a Man About a Horse – Going for a pee.

Gold Watch - Cockney Rhyming Slang for 'scotch'.

Goldie Hawn - Cockney Rhyming Slang for 'porn'.

Go Like the Clappers – Run like hell. Work hard.

Gone For a Burton – All broken, busted up.

Go Off on One – Tear someone off a strip, dress someone down, get really angry with someone and bawl them out.

Good Egg – Good person.

Good Crack – Good conversation.

Good Innings – Having a good life.

Good Rollicking – Being punished.

Good Seeing To – being beaten, in a fight, usually.

Good Value - This is short for good value for money. It means something is a good deal.

Goolies – male front lower body parts. (Ging-gang Goolies) Testicles. If you have been kicked in the goolies, your eyes would be watering and you would be clutching your balls!

Gooseberry Puddin' - Cockney Rhyming Slang for 'woman'.

Goose's Neck - Cockney Rhyming Slang for 'cheque'.

Gordon & Gotch - Cockney Rhyming Slang for 'watch'.

Gordon Bennet – Exclamation of shock. God Blimey, Good God!

Gordon Brown - Cockney Rhyming Slang for 'clown'. (Source, politician)

Gorky Park - Cockney Rhyming Slang for 'dark'.

Gormless - A gormless person is someone who has absolutely no clue. You would say clueless.

Go Spare – Go crazy.

Got the Hump – Feeling irked, upset.

GSCE – General Certificate of Secondary Education.

GP – General Practitioner; general doctor, unspecialized.

Graft – Work, sweat equity.

Grand – A thousand pounds.

Granny Flat - Cockney Rhyming Slang for 'twat'.

Grant Hackett - Cockney Rhyming Slang for 'jacket'.

Grass – Informant, one who tells on others.

Grass in the Park - Cockney Rhyming Slang for 'nark'.

Grasshopper - Cockney Rhyming Slang for 'copper'.

Gravy Lumps - Cockney Rhyming Slang for 'dumps'.

Greaser – Phlegm-laced spit.

Greasy Spoon – Cheap or dirty café, or roadside (caravan) eatery.

Greatly Missed - Cockney Rhyming Slang for 'pissed'.

GBP – Great British Pounds.

Green Eggs & Ham - Cockney Rhyming Slang for 'Exam'.

Greenfingers – Person who's good in the garden.

Greengages - Cockney Rhyming Slang for 'wages'.

Greengrocer – A seller of vegetables.

Greet – Scottish for cry, weep.

Gregory Peck - Cockney Rhyming Slang for 'neck'.

Gregory Pecks - Cockney Rhyming Slang for 'specs'.

Grem - To spit something out, phlegm.

Grey Mare - Cockney Rhyming Slang for 'fare'.

Gringy – Dirty, greasy, smelly.

Grinning Like a Cheshire Cat – Smiling real wide; from the 'Alice in Wonderland' books.

Grizzle Guts – A moaning person, whiner, a misery-guts.

Ground Floor – The floor of a building at ground level. In the UK, the 'first floor' is one floor up from the ground.

Grub - Food. Similar to nosh. I remember my Dad calling "grub's up", when dinner was ready as a kid.

Grumble & Grunt - Cockney Rhyming Slang for 'c*nt'.

Gubbins – The internal working parts of something, a man, a machine, whatever.

Guddle – Scottish to fish with your hands, or a 'mess'.

Guff – A fart.

Guiser – Scottish for kids on Halloween. "Anything for the guisers?" Adults give sweets, kids do a song, tell a joke, etc.

Gumption – Common sense, having intelligence.

Guts For Garters – a real bad thing to hear. You're going to be held responsible.

Gutted - Really upset! Devastated.

Gutties – Underwear. Also shoes (Scottish)

Guv'nor – Person in charge.

Gypo – Gipsy, traveling person.

Gypsy Nell - Cockney Rhyming Slang for 'hell'.

Gypsy's Kiss - Cockney Rhyming Slang for 'piss'.

H IS FOR HAND SHANDY

Hacked Off – Cheesed off, fed up.

Hackit – Really ugly. (Scottish)

Hackney Marsh - Cockney Rhyming Slang for glass.

Haddock - 2nd Degree Cockney Rhyming Slang for 'motor', see below.

Haddock & Bloater - Cockney Rhyming Slang for 'motor', car, vehicle.

Had Your Card Marked – Under supervision, being watched.

Haggle - To haggle is to argue, dicker or negotiate over a price. Most people that wangle stuff are usually quite good at haggling.

Hagen Daas - Cockney Rhyming Slang for 'ass'.

Hail & Rain - Cockney Rhyming Slang for 'train'.

Hair Gel - Cockney Rhyming Slang for 'bell', or telephone call.

Hairy-Arsed – Big, hairy men.

Hairy Chest - Cockney Rhyming Slang for 'very best'.

Hairy Knees - Cockney Rhyming Slang for 'please'.

Hairy Muff - Cockney Rhyming Slang for 'fair enough'.

Hairy Toes - Cockney Rhyming Slang for 'nose'.

Hale & Hearty - Cockney Rhyming Slang for 'party'.

Hale & Pace - Cockney Rhyming Slang for 'face'. (Source, British comedy duo)

Half a Gross - Cockney Rhyming Slang for 'dose'.

Half an Oxford Scholar - Cockney Rhyming Slang for 'dollar'.

Half-Arsed – Half-assed, half done, done shoddily, a poor attempt.

Half a Mo' – Short for 'half a moment', means 'hold up', 'hold on', or 'wait'.

Half-Cut – Half drunk.

Half-Inch - Cockney Rhyming Slang for 'pinch', steal.

Half Mast – Trousers not touching socks.

Ham & Cheesy - Cockney Rhyming Slang for 'easy'.

Ham & Egger - Cockney Rhyming Slang for 'beggar'.

Ham & Eggs - Cockney Rhyming Slang for 'legs'.

Hame – Home. (Scottish)

Hammer & Tack - Cockney Rhyming Slang for 'back'.

Hammered – Very drunk.

Hampden Roar - Cockney Rhyming Slang for 'score', jist, what's going on. (Source, Scottish national football ground)

Hampstead Heath - Cockney Rhyming Slang for 'teeth'.

Hampton Wick - Cockney Rhyming Slang for 'prick', penis.

Ham Shanks - Cockney Rhyming Slang for 'yanks', or 'wanks'.

Handbags at Dawn – A rather limp version of a fist-fight, in which there's more bluster than punches thrown.

Hand Shandy – Male masturbation.

Hank & Lee – 2nd Degree Cockney Rhyming Slang for 'starving'. Hank Marvin, Lee Marvin, both rhyming parts dropped.

Hanky Panky – Hanky Panky - or "slap and tickle" as some older folks call it - would be making out (or more) in America. Also used when a person is up to no good.

Hank Marvin - Cockney Rhyming Slang for 'starving'. (Source, guitarist with band Shadows)

Hans Blix - Cockney Rhyming Slang for 'fix'.

Hansel & Gretel - Cockney Rhyming Slang for 'kettle'.

Happen – Yorkshire for 'perhaps'.

Happy Feed - Cockney Rhyming Slang for 'weed', dope, drugs.

Hard – A tough aggressive male who thinks he's good at fighting, usually helped by alcohol.

Hard Cheese – Hard luck, also hard lines.

Hard Lines - This is another way of saying hard luck or bad luck.

Hard Nut – A person who is, or considers themselves to be a good fighter, or difficult to put down, very determined.

Harley Street – The street in London associated with very high-end doctors.

Harold Wilsons - Cockney Rhyming Slang for 'Stilsons', pipe wrench.

Harpers & Queens - Cockney Rhyming Slang for 'jeans', denims.

Harris Tweed - Cockney Rhyming Slang for 'weed'.

Harry & Billy - Cockney Rhyming Slang for 'silly'. (Source, sons of Princess Diana)

Harry Dash - Cockney Rhyming Slang for 'flash'.

Harry Flint - Cockney Rhyming Slang for 'skint', broke.

Harry Hill - Cockney Rhyming Slang for 'pill', usually contraceptive. (Source, British comedian)

Harry Holt - Cockney Rhyming Slang for 'bolt', run away.

Harry Lime - Cockney Rhyming Slang for 'time'.

Harry Lin - Cockney Rhyming Slang for 'chin'.

Harry Monk - Cockney Rhyming Slang for 'spunk', sperm, also 'skunk'.

Harry Potter - Cockney Rhyming Slang for 'snotter', bogled nose.

Harry Randall - Cockney Rhyming Slang for 'candle'.

Harry Tate - Cockney Rhyming Slang for 'state'.

Harry Tate – 2nd Degree Cockney Rhyming Slang for 'sugar'. (Source, Tate & Lyle sugar brand)

Harry Worth - Cockney Rhyming Slang for 'turf'. (Source, British comedian)

Harry Wragg - Cockney Rhyming Slang for 'fag', cigarette.

Harvey Nichols - Cockney Rhyming Slang for 'pickles'.

Hat & Scarf - Cockney Rhyming Slang for 'laugh'.

Hatti Jaques (Jakes) - Cockney Rhyming Slang for 'shakes'. (Source, British comedienne)

Hat Trick – One person scoring three goals in one football (soccer) game.

Haugh – Scottish for meadow by a river.

Have – Get.

Have a Butchers – Second degree Cockney Rhyming Slang (when the rhyming part has been dropped) for 'a look', originally from Butcher's Hook.

Have It Off – Have sex.

Have Your Collar Felt – Means picked up by the police... literally by the collar.

Haver – Scottish; to waffle, to talk a lot, but not say very much, or to go on about something until everyone's bored.

Having it Large – Gorging yourself on anything.

Having Kittens – Getting into an excited, upset state.

Hawd yer Wheesht – be quiet. (Scottish)

Hawking Up – Spitting.

Hay Stack - Cockney Rhyming Slang for 'back'.

Haywards Heath - Cockney Rhyming Slang for 'teeth'.

Headcase - An idiot, one who thinks he's more than he is.

Head-The-Ball – An idiot, one who thinks he's more than he is.

Heap of Coke - Cockney Rhyming Slang for 'bloke', guy.

Hearts of Oak - Cockney Rhyming Slang for 'broke'.

Heave Ho – throwing something away, also ending a relationship. "I gave her the heave-ho."

Heavenly Bliss - Cockney Rhyming Slang for 'kiss'.

Heavin' – Full, busy.

Hedge & Ditch - Cockney Rhyming Slang for 'pitch', stand, stall.

Hemming and Hawing – Indecisive.

Hen Night – Bachelorette party.

Henry Moore - Cockney Rhyming Slang for 'door'.

Henry Neville - Cockney Rhyming Slang for 'devil'.

Henry the Eighth - Cockney Rhyming Slang for 'eighth of coke'. 2nd Degree Cockney Rhyming Slang; "Cut me out an 'Enry".

Her Indoors – The wife.

Her Majesty's Pleasure - In prison.

Herring Bone - Cockney Rhyming Slang for 'phone'.

Hey Diddle Diddle - Cockney Rhyming Slang for 'fiddle'.

HMRC – Her Majesty's Revenue & Customs.

HMS – Her Majesty's Ship.

Hickory Docks - Cockney Rhyming Slang for 'socks'.

Hiding to Nothing – Nothing to be gained.

Higgledy Piggledy – All mixed up.

Highland Fling - Cockney Rhyming Slang for 'ring'.

High Tea – Small meal before dinner, usually tea and cakes.

Hilary Swank - Cockney Rhyming Slang for 'wank', masturbate.

Hillman Hunters - Cockney Rhyming Slang for 'punters'. (Source, 60's British car)

Him Indoors – The husband.

Hirple – Scottish for limp.

Hit & Miss - Cockney Rhyming Slang for 'miss', 'kiss', and 'piss'.

His Nibs – Upper class person (or one who thinks he is).

Hiya - Short for hi there, this is a friendly way of saying hello.

Hoachin' – Busy, full.

Hobson's Choice - Cockney Rhyming Slang for 'voice'.

Hobson's Choice – Having no choice at all.

Hockey Puck - Cockney Rhyming Slang for 'f*ck'.

Hogmanay – Scottish; 31st December, 'Old Year's Day'.

Hoity Toity – Having airs and graces.

Holborn Viaduct - Cockney Rhyming Slang for 'f*cked'.

Holiday Camp – Organised holiday camp, Butlins, Pontins etc.

Holler Boys Holler - Cockney Rhyming Slang for 'collar'.

Holly Wreath - Cockney Rhyming Slang for 'teeth'.

Holy Friar - Cockney Rhyming Slang for 'liar'.

Holy Ghost - Cockney Rhyming Slang for 'toast'.

Holy Grail - Cockney Rhyming Slang for 'email'.

Home & Away - Cockney Rhyming Slang for 'gay', homosexual.

Honey Bees - Cockney Rhyming Slang for 'keys'.

Hong Kong Fooey - Cockney Rhyming Slang for 'fluey' (having flu symptoms). (Source, British cartoon)

Honkin' – Smelly, stinking.

Honking (up) - Being sick or throwing up.

Hoolit – Scottish for 'owl'.

Hopping Pot - Cockney Rhyming Slang for 'lot'.

Horlicks – Hot bedtime milky drink.

Horse & Cart - Cockney Rhyming Slang for 'fart', 'tart', or 'heart'.

Horse & Trap - Cockney Rhyming Slang for 'crap'.

Horses For Courses – Something that works for some people, and not others.

Horse's Hoof - Cockney Rhyming Slang for 'roof', or 'poof'.

Hot Cross Bun - Cockney Rhyming Slang for 'nun'.

Hot Potato ('Potater') - Cockney Rhyming Slang for 'waiter'.

Hound – Derogatory term for ugly woman, girl.

Houndslow Heath - Cockney Rhyming Slang for 'teeth'.

House to Let - Cockney Rhyming Slang for 'bet'.

Housemaid's Knee - Cockney Rhyming Slang for 'sea'.

Housewives Choice - Cockney Rhyming Slang for 'voice'. (Source, British radio show)

Hovis – Bread.

Hovis – 3rd Degree Cockney Rhyming Slang for 'dead'. (Source, Brown Bread = 'dead'. Hovis is a brand of brown bread. We drop the whole first phrase, substitute it with 'Hovis'. Eg; "I thought my days were up, Hovis, mate".)

How Do You Do? – An initial greeting.

How Do You Do - Cockney Rhyming Slang for 'shoe'.

Howfin' – Smelly, stinking.

Howk – Scottish for dig.

How's It Hanging? – An initial greeting, enquiry.

How's Your Father? – Sex.

How's Your Father? - Cockney Rhyming Slang for 'lather'.

HP Brown (Broon) Sauce – Like steak sauce, but way better.

HP Fruity Sauce – Like steak sauce mixed with ketchup, but way better.

Huckelberry Finn - Cockney Rhyming Slang for 'pin'.

Hugo Boss - Cockney Rhyming Slang for 'doss', sleep.

Humdinger – Scottish slang for a great thing, woman, goal, building.

Hump - In a bad mood, also having sex.

Humpty – In a bad mood, also broken.

Hunky-Dory – Fine, groovy, no worries.

Hunty Gowk – Scottish for April Fool's day.

Hurricane Lamp - Cockney Rhyming Slang for 'tramp'.

Hydraulics - Cockney Rhyming Slang for 'bollocks'.

Ian Beale - Cockney Rhyming Slang for 'real'. (Source, Soap Opera character)

Ian Rush - Cockney Rhyming Slang for 'brush'. (Source, Welsh footballer)

Ian Wright - Cockney Rhyming Slang for 'shite'. (Source, English footballer)

Ice Cream Freezer - Cockney Rhyming Slang for 'geezer'.

Ice Lolly – Popsicle.

Ice Rink - Cockney Rhyming Slang for 'drink'.

Icing Sugar – Fine confectioners' sugar.

Ickle – Small, little.

Identity Parade – Police line-up.

Ille Nastase - Cockney Rhyming Slang for 'khazi' toilet. (Source, tennis player)

I'm Afloat - Cockney Rhyming Slang for 'coat'.

I'm easy - This expression means I don't care or it's all the same to me. Not to be confused with how easy it is to lure the person into bed!

In and Out - Cockney Rhyming Slang for 'gout', snout' (cigarette), 'kraut' (German).

Inky Smudge - Cockney Rhyming Slang for 'judge'.

Innit – Isn't it.

Insects & Ants - Cockney Rhyming Slang for 'pants'.

Inspector Morse - Cockney Rhyming Slang for 'sauce'. (Source, Fictional British detective)

Inspector Taggart - Cockney Rhyming Slang for 'faggot', homosexual. (Source, Fictional Scottish detective)

InterCity - Cockney Rhyming Slang for 'kitty', cash.

In the Nude - Cockney Rhyming Slang for 'food'.

In the (Pudding) Club – Pregnant.

In the Sack – In bed with.

Inverted Commas – Quotation marks. These… " ".

Irish Jig - Cockney Rhyming Slang for 'wig'.

Irish Rose - Cockney Rhyming Slang for 'nose'.

Irn Bru – Best-selling soda in Scotland, tastes like yummy bubble-gum, colored clear orange.

Iron Hoof - Cockney Rhyming Slang for 'poof', homosexual.

Iron Horse - Cockney Rhyming Slang for 'toss'. 2nd Degree Cockney Rhyming Slang. "I don't give an Iron, mate". (having dropped the rhyme).

Iron Lung - Cockney Rhyming Slang for 'tongue'.

Ironmonger – hardware store.

Irony/sarcasm - The cornerstones of British humour. This is one of the biggest differences between the nations. The sense of humour simply doesn't translate too well.

Iron Tank - Cockney Rhyming Slang for 'bank', wank'.

Isle of Wight - Cockney Rhyming Slang for 'right'.

I Suppose - Cockney Rhyming Slang for 'nose'.

It Be Reet – Yorkshire for 'it'll be alright'.

Itchy Ring - Cockney Rhyming Slang for 'Burger King'.

Itchy Teeth (Teef) - Cockney Rhyming Slang for 'beef'.

Ivory Band - Cockney Rhyming Slang for 'hand'.

J IS FOR JAMMIES

J. Arthur Rank – Cockney Rhyming Slang for 'bank, 'wank'. Rank was a film magnate in the 60's.

Jabba the Hutt - Cockney Rhyming Slang for 'shut'.

Jack & Dandy - Cockney Rhyming Slang for 'handy'.

Jack & Jill – Cockney Rhyming Slang for 'contraceptive pill', 'hill', 'till', 'bill'.

Jackanory – Cockney Rhyming Slang for 'story'.

Jack Dash - Cockney Rhyming Slang for 'slash', piss.

Jackdaw – Cockney Rhyming Slang for 'jaw', talk, blether.

Jack Dee - Cockney Rhyming Slang for 'cup of tea'. (Source, British comedian)

Jackie Chan – Cockney Rhyming Slang for 'plan', 'can', beer.

Jackie Danny – Cockney Rhyming Slang for 'fanny'.

Jackie Flint – Cockney Rhyming Slang for 'skint', broke.

Jack In – Stop doing something, stop work.

Jack Joner - Cockney Rhyming Slang for 'loner'.

Jack Jones – Cockney Rhyming Slang for 'on your own'. (origins; singer)

Jack McGraw - Cockney Rhyming Slang for 'draw', cannabis.

Jack Palance - Cockney Rhyming Slang for 'dance'.

Jack Straw - Cockney Rhyming Slang for 'draw', cannabis.

Jack Tar - Cockney Rhyming Slang for 'bar'.

Jack's Alive – Cockney Rhyming Slang for 'five'.

Jacksie – Your backside.

Jackson Pollocks – Cockney Rhyming Slang for 'bollocks'.

Jack the Dandy – Cockney Rhyming Slang for 'brandy'.

Jack the Lad – A male who is overly, too masculine.

Jack the Ripper – Cockney Rhyming Slang for 'kipper', smoked haddock, also 'stripper'.

Jack the Rippers – Cockney Rhyming Slang for 'slippers'.

Jack Up – To inject drugs.

Jacobs Crackers – Cockney Rhyming Slang for 'knackers', testicles. (origins; wafer bread)

Jaffa – An infertile man.

Jaffa Cake – Cockney Rhyming Slang for 'mistake'. 2nd Degree Cockney Rhyming Slang; "I made a right Jaffa there, mate".

Jah Rule – Cockney Rhyming Slang for 'school'.

Jakki Brambles – Cockney Rhyming Slang for 'shambles'. (origins; disc jockey)

Jalouse – Scottish for guess.

James Blunt – Cockney Rhyming Slang for 'c*nt'.

Jammed Brown – Cockney Rhyming Slang for 'frown'.

James Dean – Cockney Rhyming Slang for 'keen'.

James Hunt – Cockney Rhyming Slang for 'c*nt'.

Jammies – Pyjamas.

Jammy - Really lucky or flukey, fortunate.

Jam Butty – Cockney Rhyming Slang for 'nutty', crazy.

Jam Jar – Cockney Rhyming Slang for 'car'.

Jam Packed – Full to capacity.

Jam Roll – Cockney Rhyming Slang for 'arsehole', 'dole', 'Pole'.

Jam Sandwich – Police car.

Jam Tart – Cockney Rhyming Slang for 'fart', 'heart'.

Jam Tart – Heart of Midlothian (Edinburgh) soccer supporter.

Jan Leeming – Cockney Rhyming Slang for 'steaming', drunk. (origins; newscaster)

Jane Fonda – Cockney Rhyming Slang for 'wander'.

Jap's Eye – The hole at the end of a penis.

Jasper – Wasp.

Jaspered – In a mess, messed up, screwed up.

Jaw-Jaw – Talking.

Jay Kay – Cockney Rhyming Slang for 'take away'.

Jay Z – Cockney Rhyming Slang for 'cup of tea'.

Jazz Band – Cockney Rhyming Slang for 'hand'.

Jean & Norma – Cockney rhyming slang for 'Chicken Korma', type of Indian Curry.

Jean Claude van Damme – Cockney Rhyming Slang for 'spam'.

Jedi Knight – Cockney Rhyming Slang for 'shite'.

Jeff Beck – Cockney Rhyming Slang for 'neck'.

Jeffrey Dahmer – Cockney Rhyming Slang for 'charmer'.

Jekyll & Hyde – Cockney Rhyming Slang for 'snide', (fake, forgery), also 'strides', trousers.

Jellied Eel – Cockney Rhyming Slang for 'squeal', tell tales, also, 'fee', 'deal'.

Jelly – Jello.

Jelly Babies – Rubbery, jelly fruit sweets.

Jelly Bone – Cockney Rhyming Slang for 'phone'.

Jelly Roll Blues – Cockney Rhyming Slang for 'news(paper)'.

Jelly Tot – Cockney Rhyming Slang for 'spot', pluke. (origins; British confectionery)

Jenny Lee – Cockney Rhyming Slang for 'flea'.

Jennie Powell – Cockney Rhyming Slang for 'trowel'.

Jenson Button – Cockney Rhyming Slang for 'mutton'.

Jeremiah – Cockney Rhyming Slang for 'fire'.

Jeremy Beadle – Cockney Rhyming Slang for 'needle'.

Jeremy Hunt – Cockney Rhyming Slang for 'c*nt'.

Jeremy Kiles – Cockney Rhyming Slang for 'piles'.

Jerry Cottle – Cockney Rhyming Slang for 'bottle'.

Jerry-Rigged (Built) – Cobbled together, not well-made at all.

Jerry O'Gorman – Cockney Rhyming Slang for 'Mormon'.

Jerry Springer – Cockney Rhyming Slang for 'minger', not a good looking woman.

Jessie (Jessy) – Scottish for a weak or effeminate man.

Jet Fighter – Cockney Rhyming Slang for 'all-nighter'.

Jet Lag – Cockney Rhyming Slang for 'fag'.

Jet Li – Cockney Rhyming Slang for 'pee'.

Jethro Tull – Cockney Rhyming Slang for 'skull'.

Jiggery Pokery – Underhand, a secret deal, not according to the rules.

Jim Bob Babs – Cockney Rhyming Slang for 'crabs', STD.

Jim Fenner – Cockney Rhyming Slang for 'tenner', ten pound note.

Jiminee Cricket – Cockney Rhyming Slang for 'ticket'.

Jim Jams – Pyjamas.

Jimmy - Actually short for Jimmy Riddle. i.e. I'm off for a Jimmy Riddle. Cockney rhyming slang for piddle!

Jim Skinner – Cockney Rhyming Slang for 'dinner'.

Jimmy Hendrix – Cockney Rhyming Slang for 'appendix'.

Jimmy Choo's – Cockney Rhyming Slang for 'shoes'.

Jimmy Cliff – Cockney Rhyming Slang for 'whiff', smell.

Jimmy Connors – Cockney Rhyming Slang for 'honors'. (origins; tennis player)

Jimmy Giraffe – Cockney Rhyming Slang for 'laugh'.

Jimmy Greaves – Cockney Rhyming Slang for 'theives'.

Jimmy Hill – Cockney Rhyming Slang for 'pill', 'bill'.

Jimmy Nail – Cockney Rhyming Slang for 'hell', 'jail', 'email'. (origins; British actor/singer)

Jimmy O'Goblin – Cockney Rhyming Slang for 'sovereign'.

Jimmy Riddle – Cockney Rhyming Slang for 'piddle', 'widdle', pee.

Jimmy Shand – Cockney Rhyming Slang for 'hand'. (origins; Scottish accordionist)

Jimmy White – Cockney Rhyming Slang for 'shite'. (origins; snooker player)

Jings – Gosh. (Scottish)

Jizz – Sperm.

Joanna (Joan-ner) – Cockney Rhyming Slang for 'piano'.

Jobby – A shite, excrement.

Jo Blunt – Cockney Rhyming Slang for 'c*nt'.

Jobs a Good 'Un – Job finished, complete.

Jobsworth – A petty or overly bureaucratic person or attitude.

Jock – A person from Scotland.

Jockey's Whip – Cockney Rhyming Slang for 'chip', 'kip' (sleep).

Jockland – Scotland.

Jodie Marsh – Cockney Rhyming Slang for 'harsh'.

Jodrell Bank – Cockney Rhyming Slang for 'wank', masturbate.

Joe Baxi – Cockney Rhyming Slang for 'taxi'.

Joe Blake – Cockney Rhyming Slang for 'snake', 'steak', 'cake'.

Joe Bloggs – An ordinary person.

Joe Brown – Cockney Rhyming Slang for 'town'.

Joe Daki – Cockney Rhyming Slang for 'Paki'.

Joe Hart – Cockney Rhyming Slang for 'fart'.

Joe Hook – Cockney Rhyming Slang for 'book'.

Joe Hoppers – Cockney Rhyming Slang for 'coppers', police.

Joe Rook – Cockney Rhyming Slang for 'crook'.

Joey Ramone – Cockney Rhyming Slang for 'phone'.

Jog On – Go away.

John Cleese – Cockney Rhyming Slang for 'cheese'.

John Deut – Cockney Rhyming Slang for 'beaut'.

John Dillon – Cockney Rhyming Slang for 'shilling'.

John Hop – Cockney Rhyming Slang for 'cop'.

Johnny Horner – Cockney Rhyming Slang for 'corner'.

John Major – Cockney Rhyming Slang for 'wager', 'pager'.

John McCain – Cockney Rhyming Slang for 'insane'.

Johnny Rutter – Cockney Rhyming Slang for 'butter'.

Johnny Cash – Cockney Rhyming Slang for 'hash', cannabis, also 'slash', pee.

Johnny Vaughn – Cockney Rhyming Slang for 'porn'.

Johnny – Penis.

John Skinner – Cockney Rhyming Slang for 'dinner'.

John Thomas – Penis (from Lady Chatterley's Lover)

John Wayne – Cockney Rhyming Slang for 'train'.

John West – Cockney Rhyming Slang for 'very best'.

Joiner – Carpenter.

Jolly – A trip.

Jollies – Holidays, vacation.

Jonathan King – Cockney Rhyming Slang for 'ring'.

Jonathan Ross – Cockney Rhyming Slang for 'toss'. 2nd Degree Cockney Rhyming Slang eg; "I don't give a Jonathan any more…" The original rhyme being dropped.

Jonathan Rossed – Cockney Rhyming Slang for 'lost'.

Jotter – Notebook.

Jubblies – Breasts.

Jude Law– Cockney Rhyming Slang for 'score'.

Judy Dench – Cockney Rhyming Slang for 'stench', 'bench', 'wrench'.

Jugs – Breasts.

Julian Clairy – Cockney Rhyming Slang for 'fairy'.

Julian Ray – Cockney Rhyming Slang for 'gay', homosexual.

Julius Caesar – Cockney Rhyming Slang for 'geezer', bloke.

Jumble Sale – Organised yard sale.

Jumbo Jet – Cockney Rhyming Slang for 'bet'.

Jumper – Sweater.

Jumping Jack – Cockney Rhyming Slang for 'back'.

Jumping Jack Flash – Cockney Rhyming Slang for 'cash'.

Jungle Jim – Cockney Rhyming Slang for 'Tim', Catholic person.

Junkie – A person addicted to drugs.

Jurassic Park – Cockney Rhyming Slang for 'dark'.

K IS FOR KECKS

K Y Jelly – Cockney Rhyming Slang for 'telly', television.

Kangaroo Pouch – Cockney Rhyming Slang for 'couch', sofa.

Kansas & Missouri - Cockney Rhyming Slang for 'tandoori'. (tandoori is a type of Indian Curry)

Kareem Abdul Jabbar – Cockney Rhyming Slang for 'car'.

Kat Slater – Cockney Rhyming Slang for 'later', 'catch you later'.

Kate & Sidney – Cockney Rhyming Slang for 'steak & kidney'.

Kate Moss – Cockney Rhyming Slang for 'toss'. (origins; model)

Kate Mossed – Cockney Rhyming Slang for 'lost'.

Kate Nash – Cockney Rhyming Slang for 'gash', vagina.

Kathy Burke – Cockney Rhyming Slang for 'work'. (origins; British comedienne)

Katy Price – Cockney Rhyming Slang for 'nice'.

Kecks – Underwear, y-fronts.

Keech – Scottish for shite, excrement.

Keek – Scottish slang for take a peep, take a look.

Keeker – Black eye.

Keen as Mustard – Excited, energized, really into it.

Keep Mum – keep a secret, keep your mouth shut.

Keep Your Hair On – Calm down.

Keep Your Pecker up – Stay encouraged, keep your chin up.

Keith Cheggers – Cockney Rhyming Slang for 'preggers', pregnant. (origins; disc jockey)

Keith Vaz – Cockney Rhyming Slang for 'wazz', pee.

Ken – Scottish; to know.

Ken & Barbie's – Cockney Rhyming Slang for 'Starbie's', Starbucks.

Ken Dodd – Cockney Rhyming Slang for 'odd'. (origins; British comedian)

Ken Dodds – Cockney Rhyming Slang for 'odds'.

Ken Smee – Cockney Rhyming Slang for 'pee'.

Kerb Crawler - Drive slow, looking/shopping for prostitutes.

Kerfuffle – Fight, fuss, melee.

Kermit the Frog – Cockney Rhyming Slang for 'bog', toilet', or 'wog'.

Kerry Katona – Cockney Rhyming Slang for 'boner', erection.

Kerry Packered – Cockney Rhyming Slang for 'knackered', tired.

Kevin & Linda – Cockney Rhyming Slang for 'winda', window.

Khazi - Another word for the toilet. Our version of the bathroom.

Khyber Pass – Cockney Rhyming Slang for 'arse'.

Kibosh (kybosh) – To put a stop to, to end prematurely.

Kick In – To begin something.

Kick Off – To begin, to start.

Kick the Bucket – To die.

Kidney Punch – Cockney Rhyming Slang for 'lunch'.

Kid On – To lie, usually in a friendly way.

Kiddie (Kiddy) Fiddler – A child molester.

Kikki Dee – Cockney Rhyming Slang for 'tea'. (origins; singer)

Kilkenny – Cockney Rhyming Slang for 'penny'.

Kilroy Silk – Cockney Rhyming Slang for 'milk'.

King Death – Cockney Rhyming Slang for 'breath'.

King Lear – Cockney Rhyming Slang for 'ear', 'queer', or 'beer'.

Kingdom Come – Cockney Rhyming Slang for 'bum'.

Kiosk – A booth, usually for payment at a venue.

Kip - A short sleep, forty winks, or a snooze.

Kipper – Smoked haddock.

Kirk – Church (Scottish)

Kirk Stevens – Cockney Rhyming Slang for 'evens', betting term.

Kisses & Hugs – Cockney Rhyming Slang for 'drugs'.

Kist – A chest, or box.

Kitchen Sink – Cockney Rhyming Slang for 'drink', chink' (Chinese, either person or food), 'clink', prison.

Kitchen Sink Drama – Unexciting family squabble, blown out of proportion.

Kitchen Tap – Cockney Rhyming Slang for 'Jap'.

Kith and Kin – Family, close relatives.

Knackered – Totally worn out, good for nothing, tired out.

Knees up - A dance or party.

Knee-Trembler – Having sex standing up.

Knight Rider – Cockney Rhyming Slang for 'cider'.

Knob - Yet another word for the penis.

Knobbly Knees – Cockney Rhyming Slang for 'keys'.

Knob-End – Idiot, stupid.

Knobhead – Idiot, stupid.

Knock Back – Drink or eat

Knock Off – Counterfeit, fake.

Knock up -   Make pregnant, also a meal from whatever you have hanging around in the fridge.

Knocked For Six – Smacked silly. Hit big time. Cricket term for hitting the ball out of the boundary without bouncing.

Knocked Off – Stolen, counterfeit.

Knocked Up – Pregnant.

Knocking Shop – Whorehouse.

Knock It On the Head – Stop doing something.

Knockers - Another word for breasts.

Know Your Onions – Know what you're talking about, be knowledgeable on your chosen subject.

Knuckle Duster – A loop of metal, held in the fist to make a punching weapon.

Knuckle sandwich – A fist, usually delivered to the face.

Kornikova – Cockney Rhyming Slang for 'the once over'. (origins; tennis player)

Kraut – A German.

Kuala Lumpur – Cockney Rhyming Slang for 'jumper', sweater.

Kushty – Perfect, nice.

Kuwaiti Tanker – Cockney Rhyming Slang for 'wanker'.

Kvetsh – Complain, moan, whine.

Kylie Minogues – Cockney Rhyming Slang for 'brogues' patterned shoes. (origins; singer)

Kym Marsh – Cockney Rhyming Slang for 'harsh'.

L IS FOR LAUGHING GEAR

La-Di-Da – Cockney Rhyming Slang for 'cigar', 'car', or 'star'.

Lace Onto – Cotton on to, understand.

Laddie – Boy, (Scottish)

Lady Cow – Yorkshire for lady-bird.

Lady from Bristol – Cockney Rhyming Slang for 'pistol'.

Lady Godiva – Cockney Rhyming Slang for 'fiver', five pounds.

Lady in Silk – Cockney Rhyming Slang for 'milk'.

Lady Muck – A woman having airs and graces.

Lady Mucked – Cockney Rhyming Slang for 'f*cked'.

Lager & Lime – Cockney Rhyming Slang for 'time'.

Lager Lout – A young male drinker.

Lanzarote – Cockney Rhyming Slang for 'tottie', good-looking female talent.

Lara Croft – Cockney Rhyming Slang for 'soft'.

Lardy – A fat person.

Larry Flint – Cockney Rhyming Slang for 'skint', broke.

Laugh – Cockney Rhyming Slang for 'bath'.

Laugh and a Joke – Cockney Rhyming Slang for 'smoke'.

Laugh & Titter – Cockney Rhyming Slang for 'bitter', beer.

Laughing Gear – Lips, mouth.

Laundrette – Laundramat.

Lauren Riddle – Cockney Rhyming Slang for 'piddle', pee.

Lav (Lavvy) - Short for lavatory, a toilet.

Lawn Mower – Cockney Rhyming Slang for 'blower', telephone.

Laying Hen – Cockney Rhyming Slang for 'pen'.

Lead on MacDuff – Scottish for 'lead the way'.

Leamington Spa – Cockney Rhyming Slang for 'car'.

Leave It Out – means; 'you must be joking'.

Lee Marvin – Cockney Rhyming Slang for 'starving'.

Lee van Cleef – Cockney Rhyming Slang for 'grief'.

Left Footer – Left handed, also catholic.

Left in the Lurch – Cockney Rhyming Slang for 'church'.

Left Jab – Cockney Rhyming Slang for 'cab'.

Left Luggage – place to temporarily put suitcases in railway station.

Left, right and centre - If you have been looking left, right and centre, it means you have been searching all over.

Leg it – escape, run, run away, or run for it.

Legit – Short for legitimate.

Legless – Staggering Drunk.

Leg of Lamb – Cockney Rhyming Slang for 'gramme', small measurement.

Leg Over – Sex.

Legs – eleven, bingo term.

Lemon & Dash – Cockney Rhyming Slang for 'slash', pee.

Lemon & Lime – Cockney Rhyming Slang for 'crime', 'time'.

Lemon Barley – Cockney Rhyming Slang for 'charlie', cocaine.

Lemon Curd – Cockney Rhyming Slang for 'turd', 'word'.

Lemon Squash – Cockney Rhyming Slang for 'wash'.

Lemon Squeezy – Cockney Rhyming Slang for 'easy'.

Lemon Squeezer – Cockney Rhyming Slang for 'geezer', guy.

Lemon Tart – Cockney Rhyming Slang for 'smart', cheeky.

Lemony Snicket – Cockney Rhyming Slang for 'ticket'.

Let Off – Fart.

Letter Box – Hole in your front door where the postman inserts your letters.

Leo Fender – Cockney Rhyming Slang for 'bender'.

Leo Sayer – Cockney Rhyming Slang for 'all-dayer', drinking spree. (origins; singer)

Les Dennis – Cockney Rhyming Slang for 'tennis'. (origins; British comedian)

Lesley Crowthers – Cockney Rhyming Slang for 'trousers'. (origins; British comedian)

Leslie Ash – Cockney Rhyming Slang for 'slash', pee.

Lester Piggot – Cockney Rhyming Slang for 'bigot'. (origins; jockey)

Liberty X – Cockney Rhyming Slang for 'sex'.

Life & Death – Cockney Rhyming Slang for 'breath'.

Lift – A ride in a car.

Light & Bitter – Cockney Rhyming Slang for 'shitter', arse.

Light & Dark – Cockney Rhyming Slang for 'park'.

Lightning Ridge – Cockney Rhyming Slang for 'fridge'.

Lilian Gish – Cockney Rhyming Slang for 'fish'.

Lilley & Skinner – Cockney Rhyming Slang for 'beginner', 'dinner'.

Lily Paps – Nipples.

Lily the Pink – Cockney Rhyming Slang for 'drink'.

Limehouse Link – Cockney Rhyming Slang for 'chink', Chinese.

Linen Draper – Cockney Rhyming Slang for 'newspaper'.

Lionel Bart – Cockney Rhyming Slang for 'tart'.

Lionel Blair – Cockney Rhyming Slang for 'nightmare', 'flares', trousers.

Lionel Ritchie – Cockney Rhyming Slang for 'bitchy'.

Lion's Lair – Cockney Rhyming Slang for 'chair'.

Lisa Tarbuck's – Cockney Rhyming Slang for 'Starbucks'. (origins; actress)

Listerine – 3rd degree Cockney Rhyming Slang for 'anti-American'. Septic Tank, rhymes with yank. Anti-septic, means anti-yank, Listerine is an anti-septic cream.

Little & Large – Cockney Rhyming Slang for 'marge', margarine.

Little Jack Horner – Cockney Rhyming Slang for 'corner'.

Liz Hurley – Cockney Rhyming Slang for 'early'.

Liza Minelli – Cockney Rhyming Slang for 'telly', television.

Loaf of Bread – Cockney Rhyming Slang for 'head'. "Use your loaf!", meaning "think about it".

Lollipop – Cockney Rhyming Slang for 'shop'.

Lollipop man – Person who stops traffic to let children cross the road safely. His sign looks like a lollipop.

Lolly – Money, cash.

Lolly Lick – Cockney Rhyming Slang for 'prick', 'dick', penis.

London Fog – Cockney Rhyming Slang for 'dog'.

Long & Flexy – Cockney Rhyming Slang for 'sexy'.

Long 'Un – One hundred.

Longers & Lingers – Cockney Rhyming Slang for 'fingers'.

Loo – Toilet.

Looby Loo's – Cockney Rhyming Slang for 'shoes'.

Looking Like a Lemon – Looking like a fool.

Loon – Young man, boy. (NE Scotland)

Loop the Loop – Cockney Rhyming Slang for 'soup'.

Lord Lovell – Cockney Rhyming Slang for 'shovel'.

Lord Mayor – Cockney Rhyming Slang for 'swear', curse.

Lord of the Manor – Cockney Rhyming Slang for 'tanner', sixpence.

Lords & Peers – Cockney Rhyming Slang for 'ears'.

Lorna Doone – Cockney Rhyming Slang for 'spoon'.

Lorry – Big truck, Tractor trailer.

Lose the Rag – Lose your temper.

Lost Property Office – Where lost items are handed in, and collected from.

Lost & Found – Cockney Rhyming Slang for 'pound', money.

Lost the Plot – Gone screwy, gone crazy, gone 'off the rails'.

Louise Wener – Cockney Rhyming Slang for 'tenner', ten pounds.

Love & Kisses – Cockney Rhyming Slang for 'missus', wife, girlfriend.

Love Bite – Hickey, hickie.

Lovely Jubbly – Great, wonderful.

Love Me Tender – Cockney Rhyming Slang for 'bender', homosexual.

Lucky Dip – Cockney Rhyming Slang for 'kip', sleep.

Lucy Locket – Cockney Rhyming Slang for 'pocket'.

Lug – Scottish for 'ear'.

Lug-hole – Earhole.

Lumber – guy slang for getting off, and having sex. Your girl is your lumber.

Lump It – Put up with.

Lump of Lead – Cockney Rhyming Slang for 'head'.

Lurgy – Stomach illness, illness, Flu.

Lush – Lovely, pretty, also a big spender/looker.

M IS FOR MESSAGES

M&S - Short for Marks & Spencer (department store).

Mac – Short for Mackintosh, raincoat.

Maca – 3rd Degree Cockney Rhyming Slang for 'crap'. Macaroni- pony. Pony & Trap – crap.

Macaroni – Cockney Rhyming Slang for 'pony', 25 pounds.

Macaroni Cheese – Cockney Rhyming Slang for 'keys'.

Macca – Paul McCartney.

Made Redundant – Paid off, with a monetary leaving package.

Mad For It – Eager for, liking something.

Made a Fist of Things – Made a mess.

Mae West – Cockney Rhyming Slang for 'best'.

Maggie's Den – Cockney Rhyming Slang for 'number 10', Downing Street.

Magic – Good, excellent, great.

Magnus Pike – Cockney Rhyming Slang for 'dyke', lesbian.

Mahatma Ghandi – Cockney Rhyming Slang for 'brandy', 'shandy'.

Mailed and Sent – Cockney Rhyming Slang for 'bent', homosexual.

Mains – Direct water supply (not from a tank).

Maist – Most. (Scottish)

Major Loda – Cockney Rhyming Slang for 'soda'.

Major Stevens – Cockney Rhyming Slang for 'evens', betting term.

Make it Snappy – Do it quickly, (usually an instruction).

Make Mincemeat of somebody (something) – Hammer them senseless, beat into submission, complete the job easily.

Mal Maninga – Cockney Rhyming Slang for 'finger'.

Malcolm in the Middle – Cockney Rhyming Slang for 'piddle', pee.

Malcolm X – Cockney Rhyming Slang for 'text', message.

Malky Fraser – Cockney Rhyming Slang for 'razor'.

Mam – Breasts.

Mammeries – Breasts.

Mammy's Smiles – Cockney Rhyming Slang for 'piles', hemorrhoids.

Mancunian – Someone from Manchester.

Mandy Dingle – Cockney Rhyming Slang for 'single'.

Mandy Dingles – Cockney Rhyming Slang for 'shingles'.

Manfred Mann – Cockney Rhyming Slang for 'plan'.

Man From Cairo – Cockney Rhyming Slang for 'giro', dole payment.

Manhole Cover – Cockney Rhyming Slang for 'brother'.

Manky – Dirty, gross, clarty, disgusting.

Manor – Your home, house

Mantelpiece – The shelf above a fireplace.

Mariah Carey – Cockney Rhyming Slang for 'scary'.

Marie Correlli – Cockney Rhyming Slang for 'telly', television.

Marilyn Manson – Cockney Rhyming Slang for 'handsome'.

Marilyn Monroes – Cockney Rhyming Slang for 'toes'.

Market Stalls – Cockney Rhyming Slang for 'balls', testicles'.

Mark Ramprakash – Cockney Rhyming Slang for 'slash', pee. (origins; cricketer)

Marks & Sparks - Marks & Spencer (department store)

Marquis de Sade – Cockney Rhyming Slang for 'hard', erection.

Mars & Venus – Cockney Rhyming Slang for 'penis'.

Mars Bar – Cockney Rhyming Slang for 'scar'.

Marty Pellow – Cockney Rhyming Slang for 'yellow'. (origins; singer)

Martial Arts – Cockney Rhyming Slang for 'darts'.

Martin Kemp – Cockney Rhyming Slang for 'hemp', drugs.

Martini – Cockney Rhyming Slang for 'Lambourghini'.

Mary Rose – Cockney Rhyming Slang for 'nose'.

Master McGrath – Cockney Rhyming Slang for 'bra'.

Mate – Friend, pal, chum.

Maths – Math.

Matt le Tiss – Cockney Rhyming Slang for 'piss'. (origins; Matt le Tissier, footballer)

Matthew Kelly – Cockney Rhyming Slang for 'telly', television, or 'belly'.

Maurice Gibb – Cockney Rhyming Slang for 'fib'.

Mawkit – Dirty. (Scottish)

Me & You – Cockney Rhyming Slang for 'menu'.

Meat and Two Veg – Men's genitalia, all parts.

Mechanical Digger – Cockney Rhyming Slang for 'nigger'.

Melody Lingers – Cockney Rhyming Slang for 'fingers'.

Meltit – Drunk. (Scottish)

Melvyn Bragg – Cockney Rhyming Slang for 'shag'.

Mensch – Important person.

Merchant Banker – Cockney Rhyming Slang for 'wanker'.

Merchant Navy – Cockney Rhyming Slang for 'gravy'.

Merlyn Rees – Cockney Rhyming Slang for 'piece', sandwich.

Merry – Mildly drunk.

Merryheart – Cockney Rhyming Slang for 'tart'.

Meryl Streep – Cockney Rhyming Slang for 'cheap'.

Messages – Groceries, shopping.

Metal Mickey – Cockney Rhyming Slang for 'sickie', sick day.

Metric Miles – Cockney Rhyming Slang for 'piles', hemorrhoids.

Mexican Wave – Cockney Rhyming Slang for 'shave'.

Michael Caine – Cockney Rhyming Slang for 'pain'.

Michael Miles – Cockney Rhyming Slang for 'piles', hemorrhoids.

Michael Schumachers – Cockney Rhyming Slang for 'knackers', testicles.

Michael Winner – Cockney Rhyming Slang for 'dinner'.

Mick Jagger – Cockney Rhyming Slang for 'lager'.

Mickey Duff – Cockney Rhyming Slang for 'puff', of marijuana.

Mickey Monk – Cockney Rhyming Slang for 'drunk'.

Mickey Most – Cockney Rhyming Slang for 'toast'.

Mickey Mouse – Cockney Rhyming Slang for 'house', 'scouse' (coming from Liverpool).

Mickey Rourke – Cockney Rhyming Slang for 'pork'.

Midden – A mess, disgusting.

Middling – Moderate, average.

Midland Bank – Cockney Rhyming Slang for 'wank', masturbate.

Miffed – Upset, annoyed.

Mikkel Becks – Cockney Rhyming Slang for 'specs', glasses.

Milky Way – Cockney Rhyming Slang for 'gay', homosexual.

Mileometer – Trip reader in a car.

Milk Float – Truck that delivers milk to the door.

Millwall in Riot – Cockney Rhyming Slang for 'pirate'.

Milton Keynes – Cockney Rhyming Slang for 'jeans', denims.

Mince – Rubbish, also ground beef.

Mince Around – Waste time, work shoddily/slowly.

Mince Pie – Ground beef pie.

Mince Pies – Cockney Rhyming Slang for 'eyes'.

Mind – Pay attention, watch what you're doing. "Oy, mind where you're walking!"

Mind your P's and Q's – Have good manners, be on best behaviour.

Minder – Bodyguard.

Minging – Smelly, ugly, disgusting, horrible.

Mink – A dirty person.

Minnie Driver – Cockney Rhyming Slang for 'fiver', five pounds.

Minted – Rich, wealthy.

Missing Link – Cockney Rhyming Slang for 'chink', Chinese.

Mitt – Hand.

MOD – Ministry of Defence.

MOT – Ministry of Transport.

Mo – Short for 'moment'.

Moaning Minnie – A complaining person, whiner, moaner.

Mob Handed – In a bunch, a gang, not alone. "When the gang arrived, mob-handed, we legged it smartish."

Moby Dick – Cockney Rhyming Slang for 'prick', penis, or 'sick'.

Mods & Rockers – Cockney Rhyming Slang for 'knockers', boobs.

Molly Malone – Cockney Rhyming Slang for 'phone'.

Molly O'Morgan – Cockney Rhyming Slang for 'organ'.

Molten Toffee – Cockney Rhyming Slang for 'coffee'.

Momentarily - A very short space of time. "I'll be there momentarily".

Money Pits – Cockney Rhyming Slang for 'stripper's tits'.

Monkey – 500 pounds (money).

Monkey Wrench – Cockney Rhyming Slang for 'wench'.

Monkey's Tails – Cockney Rhyming Slang for 'nails'.

Montey's Army – Cockney Rhyming Slang for 'barmy'.

Montezuma's Revenge – Diarrhoea.

Moo – An ugly person.

Moo-Poo – Bullshit.

Mooch – Cadge, ask for stuff, beg for. Also saunter, slow dithering walk.

Moolah – Money, cash.

Moose – Scottish slang for mouse.

Mooth – Scottish slang for mouth.

Mop & Broom – Cockney Rhyming Slang for 'Fruit of the Loom'.

Morecombe & Wise – Cockney Rhyming Slang for 'flies'. (origins; comedians)

Moriarty – Cockney Rhyming Slang for 'party'.

Mor-ish (More-ish) – More, a small amount more.

Mork & Mindy – Cockney Rhyming Slang for 'windy'.

Morning Glory – Cockney Rhyming Slang for 'story'.

Morris Minor – Cockney Rhyming Slang for 'vagina'. (origins; car)

Mother & Daughter – Cockney Rhyming Slang for 'quarter'.

Mother Goose – Cockney Rhyming Slang for 'loose'.

Mother Hubbard – Cockney Rhyming Slang for 'cupboard'.

Mother of Pearl – Cockney Rhyming Slang for 'girl'.

Mother's Ruin – Gin.

Mountain Bike – Cockney Rhyming Slang for 'dyke', lesbian.

Mozambique – Cockney Rhyming Slang for 'keek', peep.

Mrs Chant – Cockney Rhyming Slang for 'aunt'.

Mrs Duckett – Cockney Rhyming Slang for 'bucket'.

Muck Around – Horse around, not be serious.

Muck In – Work hard, help, give assistance.

Muck Up – Mess up, make a mess of.

Mucker – Friend, pal.

Mucky Pup – Derogatory term, dirty/disliked person.

Muff Diver – Cockney Rhyming Slang for 'fiver', five pounds.

Mufti - An old army term for your "civvies". Civilian clothes that is, rather than your uniform.

Mug – Gullible person, also to rob/attack.

Muggins – Me. "Who turned up, huh, just me, muggins."

Mug's Game – Situation in which a gullible person is taken advantage of.

Mum & Dad – Cockney Rhyming Slang for 'mad'.

Muppet – Idiot, silly, stupid person.

Murray Mint – Cockney Rhyming Slang for 'skint', broke.

Mush - Slang word for your mouth, "shut your mush". Also friend, mate.

Mushy Peas – Cockney Rhyming Slang for 'keys'.

Mustard – Real good, excellent.

Muswell Hill – Cockney Rhyming Slang for 'bill'.

Mutt and Jeff – Cockney Rhyming Slang for 'deaf'.

Mutter & Stutter – Cockney Rhyming Slang for 'butter'.

Mutton Dressed as Lamb – An older person dressed up in a younger look.

Mutt's Nuts - Another way of saying "Dog's Bollocks"! Means fantastic or excellent.

My Ansum – Yorkshire for 'my friend'.

Myleen Class – Cockney Rhyming Slang for 'arse'.

Mystic Megs – Cockney Rhyming Slang for 'legs'.

N IS FOR NUTTER

Naff – Not good, poor quality, bad.

Naff Off – Means 'get lost'.

Nails & Tacks – Cockney Rhyming Slang for 'fax'.

Nancy Boy – An effeminate man, also a gay man.

Nanny Goat – Cockney Rhyming Slang for 'throat', 'boat', 'tote', 'coat'.

Naomi Campbell – Cockney Rhyming Slang for 'gamble'.

Nat King Cole – Cockney Rhyming Slang for 'dole', welfare, or 'hole', as in "Did you get your hole last night?" (Did you get to have sex?)

Nappie (Nappy) – Daiper.

Nark – To annoy someone, get on their nerves. Also a stool pigeon, an informer.

Narked - In a bad mood.

Native New Yorker – Cockney Rhyming Slang for 'porker', fat person.

Natter – Chat.

Naughts and Crosses - Checkers.

Near & Far – Cockney Rhyming Slang for 'car', bar'.

Near the Knuckle – Usually speech, comments; very rude, very blue.

NED – Non-Educated Delinquent; an uncultured, low class person.

Needle & Pin – Cockney Rhyming Slang for 'gin'.

Ne'erday – Scottish slang for New Year's Day, 1st January.

Neil Sedaka – Cockney Rhyming Slang for 'parka', jacket.

Nelly Duff – Cockney Rhyming Slang for 'puff', (life). "Not on your puff!"

Nelson Mandela – Cockney Rhyming Slang for 'pint of Stella'.

Nelson Eddie's – Cockney Rhyming Slang for 'readies', cash money.

Nervo – Nine.

Nervo & Knox – Cockney Rhyming Slang for 'pox', also 'goggle box', television.

Nervous Wreck – Cockney Rhyming Slang for 'cheque', 'check'.

Nesh – A wimp.

Netty – Scottish for 'toilet'.

Neves – Seven (backwards).

New Delhi – Cockney Rhyming Slang for 'belly'.

Newgate Jail – Cockney Rhyming Slang for 'tale'.

Newington Butts – Cockney Rhyming Slang for 'guts'.

Niagara Falls – Cockney Rhyming Slang for 'balls', testicles.

Nice Little Earner – A good paying job.

Nice one! – An affirmative/positive expression.

Nick – Jailhouse, prison, or 'steal'.

Nick - To nick is both to steal or arrest someone… so if you nick something you might well get nicked.

Nick Cotton – Cockney Rhyming Slang for 'rotten'. (origins; bad guy soap character)

Nicked - Something that has been stolen has been nicked. Also, when a copper catches a burglar red handed he might say "you've been nicked"!

Nicker – Slang for British pound.

Nicky Lauder – Cockney Rhyming Slang for 'powder', cocaine.

Nifty – Cockney Rhyming Slang for 'fifty'.

Nigel Benn – Cockney Rhyming Slang for 'ten', pounds.

Nigel Mansell – Cockney Rhyming Slang for 'cancel'.

Niggling – Annoying, never giving up.

Nightboat to Cairo – Cockney Rhyming Slang for 'giro', method of payment of unemployment benefit.

Nig-nog - An old/derogatory expression for a person of black skin.

Nina Simone – Cockney Rhyming Slang for 'phone'.

Ninepence to the Shilling – Backward, not clever, having something missing.

Nipper – Child.

Nippin' – Stinging, sore. (Scottish)

Nits – Head lice

Nitwit – Idiot, silly person.

Noah's Ark – Cockney Rhyming Slang for 'shark', 'park'.

Nobbled – Broken, not working, sabotaged.

Nobby Stiles – Cockney Rhyming Slang for 'piles', hemorrhoids.

Noddy Holders – Cockney Rhyming Slang for 'shoulders'.

Noggin – Your head… "he's off his noggin!"

No Hope – Cockney Rhyming Slang for 'soap'.

No Joy – No luck, no success.

Nonce – A pedophile, a person having too much interest in children.

Nookie – Sex, hanky panky.

North & South – Cockney Rhyming Slang for 'mouth'.

Nose & Chin – Cockney Rhyming Slang for 'gin'.

Nosebag – Food, grub.

Nosh – Food, grub.

Not a Sausage – Nothing, nil.

Not Backward at Coming Forward – A pushy, forward, confident person.

Not Batting on a Full Wicket - Backward, not clever, having something missing.

Not Cricket – Against the rules, cheating.

Not My Cup of Tea - Not to your liking. Not your kind of thing.

Not on Your Nelly – Never. Not going to happen.

Not to be Sneezed At – Not to be missed, a good opportunity.

Nowt - Yorkshire for nothing. Similarly owt is Yorkshire for anything... "you don't get owt for nowt". Roughly translated as "you never get anything for nothing".

Nuclear Sub – Cockney Rhyming Slang for 'pub'.

Nuddy – Nude.

Number Plate – Car tag.

Numpty – A stupid person, one with no sense.

Nuns & Habits – Cockney Rhyming Slang for 'rabbits'.

Nuremburg Trials – Cockney Rhyming Slang for 'piles', hemorrhoids.

Nut – Your head, also to nut someone is to head butt them.

Nutter – An idiot, a crazy person.

O IS FOR OLIVER HARDY

Oats & Barley – Cockney Rhyming Slang for 'charlie', cocaine.

Obediah – Cockney Rhyming Slang for 'fire'.

Obi Wan Kenobi – Cockney Rhyming Slang for 'mobi', mobile phone.

Obie Trice – Cockney Rhyming Slang for 'nice'.

Ocean-Going Squid – Cockney Rhyming Slang for 'quid', pound.

Ocean Pearl – Cockney Rhyming Slang for 'girl'.

Ocean Wave – Cockney Rhyming Slang for 'shave'.

Odds and Sods – Scraps, left-over parts.

Oedipus Rex – Cockney Rhyming Slang for 'sex'.

Off Colour - Looking pale and ill!

Off the Back of a Lorry – Stolen, not honestly acquired, of dubious source.

Off the Peg – Not made to measure.

Off to Bedfordshire – Going to Bed.

Off You Pop – Told to go away.

Offy – Short for 'Off licence'; a liquor store.

Off Your head – Stoned drunk.

Off Your Trolley - Bonkers, crazy, mad!

Ogden Nash – Cockney Rhyming Slang for 'slash', pee.

Oil Lamp – Cockney Rhyming Slang for 'tramp'.

Oil Rig – Cockney Rhyming Slang for 'wig'.

Oil Tanker – Cockney Rhyming Slang for 'wanker'.

Oily Rag – Cockney Rhyming Slang for 'fag'.

Old Banger – Old car.

Old Bill – Police.

Old King Cole – Cockney Rhyming Slang for 'dole', unemployment benefit.

Old Mother Hubbard – Cockney Rhyming Slang for 'cupboard'.

Old Pot & Pan – Cockney Rhyming Slang for 'old man'.

Old School – The old fashioned way.

Old Soak – An elderly alcoholic.

Oliver Hardy – Cockney Rhyming Slang for 'lardy', fat.

Oliver Twist – Cockney Rhyming Slang for 'fist', 'pissed drunk'.

OAP - Old Age Pensioner. (senior citizen)

Omar Riza – Cockney Rhyming Slang for 'pizza'.

Omar Sharif – Cockney Rhyming Slang for 'greif'.

On About – Talking about. "What are you on about?"

Once a Week – Cockney Rhyming Slang for 'cheek'.

One and T'Other – Cockney Rhyming Slang for 'brother'.

One Foot in the Grave – Very old.

One Off – One time only, a one-time event that is never to be repeated.

One For the Road – One last drink before leaving.

One Whiff of the Barmaid's Apron – A lightweight drinker, easily drunk.

One Eyed Trouser Snake – Penis.

Ones & Twos – Cockney Rhyming Slang for 'shoes'.

One Time Looker – Cockney Rhyming Slang for 'hooker'.

OHMS – On Her Majesty's Service.

Onion Bagi – Cockney Rhyming Slang for 'sargy', sergeant.

On It – Paying full attention, keeping detail.

On the Cards – Predictable.

On the Floor – Cockney Rhyming Slang for 'poor'.

On the Job - Hard at work, also having sex.

On the Lash – Drinking heavily. Out to get drunk, or to get pissed.

On the Liss - Out to get drunk, or to get pissed. Drinking heavily.

On the Piss - Out to get drunk, or to get pissed. Drinking heavily.

On the Pull – Out looking for sexual/romantic company.

On the Razzle - Drinking heavily. Out to get drunk, or to get pissed.

On the Up and Up – Going up in the world, improving.

On Your Bike - A very polite way of telling someone to f*ck off.

On Your Knees – Cockney Rhyming Slang for 'pease'.

On Your Todd – On your own.

Oppo – Workmate.

Optic Nerve – Cockney Rhyming Slang for 'perv'.

Orange & Pear – Cockney Rhyming Slang for 'swear', curse.

Orange Peel – Cockney Rhyming Slang for 'feel'.

Orcadian – Scottish slang for someone from the Orkney Islands.

Orchestra Stalls – Cockney Rhyming Slang for 'balls', testicles.

Order of the Boot – Being dismissed, sent away, off the job, given the sack.

Osama Bin Laden – Cockney Rhyming Slang for 'pardon'.

Oscar Ashe – Cockney Rhyming Slang for 'cash'.

Oscar Wilde – Cockney Rhyming Slang for 'mild'.

Otis Reading – Cockney Rhyming Slang for 'wedding', also 'head in'. "This is doing my head in!"

Our Kid – Your sibling, brother or sister.

Outings & Festivals – Cockney Rhyming Slang for 'testicles'.

Out Like a Light – Fast asleep, unconscious.

Out of Puff – Out of breath.

Oven Mitts – Cockney Rhyming Slang for 'tits', breasts.

Over the Shoulder Boulder Holder – Bra.

Owen Nares – Cockney Rhyming Slang for 'chairs'.

Owt - Yorkshire for something. Similarly nowt is Yorkshire for nothing… "you don't get owt for nowt". Roughly translated as "you never get anything for nothing".

Oxford Punt – Cockney Rhyming Slang for 'c*nt'.

Oxford Scholar – Cockney Rhyming Slang for 'collar'.

Oxo – A beef cube used to make gravy. There's two things used to make quick brown gravy in the UK, Oxo and Bisto.

Oxo Cube – Cockney Rhyming Slang for 'tube', idiot.

Oxters – Armpits.

Oyster Bay – Cockney Rhyming Slang for 'gay', homosexual.

P IS FOR PISSED AS A FART

P45 – Employment tax Form.

Packed Lunch – A lunch, packed in a bag, tin or box.

Paddy – An Irishman.

Pain In the Arse – An annoyance.

Painters and Decorators – A woman's menstrual cycle.

Paki – A Pakistani.

Paki, The – A shop owned/run by a Pakistani or anyone of 'brown' colour.

Paki-Bashing – Offensive description of slagging off, or actually fighting, beating up people of colour.

Palaver – Scottish slang for fuss.

Pam Shriver – Cockney Rhyming Slang for 'fiver, five pounds'. (origins; tennis player)

Pan – Bread with a soft crust.

Pan In – Break, smash.

Panda Car - Old blue/white police car.

Pantomime – A children's play set to music, usually at Christmas. It also describes an event that has gotten out of hand.

Pants – Underwear, panties, y-fronts.

Pants - Crap. "That last episode of Baywatch was total pants".

Paper Hat – Cockney Rhyming Slang for 'prat'.

Paper Round – A route that a paperboy/girl delivers newspapers in.

Paps – Yet another word for a woman's breasts.

Paraffin Lamp – Cockney Rhyming Slang for 'tramp'.

Paraffin Oil – Cockney Rhyming Slang for 'boil'.

Paralytic – Really drunk, so drunk, you're almost paralysed.

Pard – Short for 'pardner', means friend, pal.

Pardon Me – A polite expression of apology, (Excuse me) usually when farting, burping, belching, etc.

Park Benches – Cockney Rhyming Slang for 'Frenchies'.

Parky – Chilly, cold.

Park Your Arse – Sit down.

Park Yourself – Sit down.

Pash – Having a crush on a teacher, much older person.

Pass - This means "I don't know" and comes from the old TV show, Mastermind, where contestants were made to say "pass" if they did not know the answer to the question.

Pat & Mick – Cockney Rhyming Slang for 'sick'.

Pat Cash– Cockney Rhyming Slang for 'slash', pee.

Pat Malone – Cockney Rhyming Slang for 'alone'.

Patrick McNee – Cockney Rhyming Slang for 'wee', 'pee'.

Patrick Swayze – Cockney Rhyming Slang for 'lazy', crazy'.

Patsy Cline – Cockney Rhyming Slang for 'line', cocaine.

Paul Dickov – Cockney Rhyming Slang for 'kick off'. (origins; footballer)

Paul McKenna – Cockney Rhyming Slang for 'tenner', ten pounds. (origins; hypnotist)

Paul Weller – Cockney Rhyming Slang for 'Stella', beer.

Pauline Fowler – Cockney Rhyming Slang for 'growler', vagina.

Pavement – Sidewalk.

Pavement Pizza - A descriptive way of saying vomit. Often found outside Indian restaurants early on a Sunday morning.

Peachy – Good, excellent, great.

Peaky – Looking pale, ill, out of sorts.

Peanut Butter – Cockney Rhyming Slang for 'nutter'.

Peanuts – Cheap, inexpensive, very little money.

Pear Halved – Cockney Rhyming Slang for 'starved'.

Pearl Diver – Cockney Rhyming Slang for 'skiver, 'fiver'.

Pearly Queen – Cockney Rhyming Slang for 'seen'.

Pear Shaped – Gone wrong, become a disaster, got far worse than expected, got all out of proportion.

Peas & Gravy – Cockney Rhyming Slang for 'Navy'.

Pea Shooter – Cockney Rhyming Slang for 'hooter', nose.

Peas in the Pot – Cockney Rhyming Slang for 'hot'.

Pea Souper – Very foggy.

Pebble-Dashed – Cockney Rhyming Slang for 'smashed', drunk.

Peckham Rye – Cockney Rhyming Slang for 'tie'.

Pedal & Crank – Cockney Rhyming Slang for 'bank', 'wank'.

Pee – Urinate.

Peelers – Original slang for policemen. Police service was set up in 1829 by Sir Robert Peel.

Peelie Wally – Scottish slang for looking peaky, somewhat ill, pale, not in top shape.

Peep Scarf – Burqa (Muslim headscarf).

Pegged out – Dead.

Pelican Crossing – A place to cross the road, with lights, stop/walk signs etc.

Pelting – Really raining hard.

Pen and Ink – Cockney Rhyming Slang for 'stink'.

Penelope Cruz – Cockney Rhyming Slang for 'booze'.

Penelope Keith – Cockney Rhyming Slang for 'teeth'.

Penny a Pound – Cockney Rhyming Slang for 'ground'.

Peppermint – Cockney Rhyming Slang for 'skint', broke.

Percy Thrower – Cockney Rhyming Slang for 'mower', 'blower', telephone. (origins; gardener)

Perpetual Loser – Cockney Rhyming Slang for 'boozer', pub.

Perry Como – Cockney Rhyming Slang for 'homo'.

Persian Rugs – Cockney Rhyming Slang for 'drugs'.

Pete Tong – Cockney Rhyming Slang for 'wrong'. (origins; disc jockey)

Peter Crouch – Cockney Rhyming Slang for 'grouch'.

Peter Kay – Cockney Rhyming Slang for 'gay'.

Peter Pan – Cockney Rhyming Slang for 'old man', father.

Peter Purvis – Cockney Rhyming Slang for 'nervous'.

Petal – A term of endearment, fondness.

Peter Out – Get less and less.

Petrol – Gasoline (for cars).

Petrol Pump – Cockney Rhyming Slang for 'hump', moodiness.

Petrol Tanks – Cockney Rhyming Slang for 'Yanks'.

Philharmonic – Cockney Rhyming Slang for 'Gin & Tonic'.

Pibroch – Complicated music for bagpipes.

Piccadilly – Cockney Rhyming Slang for 'silly'.

Piccadilly Percy – Cockney Rhyming Slang for 'mercy'.

Piccolo & Flute – Cockney Rhyming Slang for 'suit'.

Pick & Mix – Cockney Rhyming Slang for 'sticks', in the countryside.

Pictures, The– The cinema.

Pie & Liquor – Cockney Rhyming Slang for 'vicar'.

Pie & Mash – Cockney Rhyming Slang for 'cash', 'slash', pee.

Piece of Cake – A cinch, easy to accomplish.

Piece of Piss - A cinch, easy to accomplish.

Pieces of Eight – Cockney Rhyming Slang for 'weight'.

Pied Piper – Cockney Rhyming Slang for 'hyper'.

Piggies – Pyjamas.

Pig Out – Eat a lot.

Pigs – Police.

Pig's Ear – A mess. "He made a right pig's ear of the decorating".

Pig's Ear – Cockney Rhyming Slang for 'beer'.

Pikey – Gypsy, Gippo. Travelling person.

Pillar Box – A red box with a slot for posting letters.

Pillock – An idiot.

Pimple & Blotch – Cockney Rhyming Slang for 'scotch', whisky.

Pimps – Easy.

Pin Pegs – Cockney Rhyming Slang for 'legs'.

Pinch - Steal, pilfer.

Pineapple – Cockney Rhyming Slang for 'chapel'.

Pineapple Chunk – Cockney Rhyming Slang for 'bunk', 'spunk'.

Pineapple Fritter – Cockney Rhyming Slang for 'shitter', arsehole.

Ping Pong – Cockney Rhyming Slang for 'strong'.

Pinky – 50 pound note.

Pinky & Perky– Cockney Rhyming Slang for 'turkey'.

Pinny – An apron; probably short for pinafore.

Pip Pip - Out-dated expression meaning goodbye.

Pipe in Your Eye – Cockney Rhyming Slang for 'cry'.

Pirate Ship – Cockney Rhyming Slang for 'full of shit'.

Pirates of Penzance – Cockney Rhyming Slang for 'pants'.

Pish – Rubbish. (Scottish) Or to pee.

Pished – Drunk. (Scottish) Or having pee'd.

Piss It Up the Wall – Usually linked to spending money on alcohol, just to piss/pee it away.

Piss Like a Racehorse – When you've been holding it in for FAR too long, and you simply have to pee NOW!

Piss Poor - Means it is an extremely poor attempt at something. Bad performance.

Piss Up - A drinking session, a visit to the pub, drinking party.

Pissed – Drunk.

Pissed as a Fart – Pretty drunk.

Pissed Off – Upset, angry about something.

Pissing Around - Fooling about, messing around.

Pissing it Down – Really raining.

Pistol & Shooter – Cockney Rhyming Slang for 'computer'.

Pitch – A grass area where ball games are played. Football pitch, rugby pitch.

Pitch & Toss – Cockney Rhyming Slang for 'boss'.

Pittsburg Steelers – Cockney Rhyming Slang for 'peelers', policemen.

Plain – Bread with a hard, burnt crust.

Plank – An idiot. So stupid he resembles a piece of wood.

Plastered – Very drunk.

Plates & Dishes – Cockney Rhyming Slang for 'missus'.

Plates of Meat – Cockney Rhyming Slang for 'feet'.

Playing Truant – Skipping/missing school or work.

Playing Silly Buggers – To fool about, lark, waste time.

Pleased as Punch – Very pleased.

Pleasure & Pain – Cockney Rhyming Slang for 'rain'.

Pleb – Lower classes.

Plimsole Mark – Cockney Rhyming Slang for 'park'.

Plimsoles - Also called 'rubbers', they're very basic training shoes.

Plod – To walk about solidly. Also slang for policemen; from a comic, P.C. Plod.

Plonk – Cheap wine or champagne.

Plonker – An idiot. Made famous in Only Fools and Horses. "You are a plonker, Rodney!"

Plymouth Argyles – Cockney Rhyming Slang for 'piles', hemorrhoids. (origins; football team)

Plymouth Sound – Cockney Rhyming Slang for 'pound'.

Pocket Watch – Cockney Rhyming Slang for 'scotch', whisky.

POET's day – Friday; Piss Off early, Tomorrow's Saturday.

Point Percy at the Porcelain – Aim the penis correctly when urinating.

Polo Mint – Cockney Rhyming Slang for 'bint', 'skint'.

Poke – To stick your finger in something, also means a paper or plastic bag.

Polis – Police. (Glasgow)

Poly Bag – Polythene bag given at supermarkets to hold groceries.

Polyfilla – Filler, spackling.

Ponce – Originally a pimp, but now also means an effeminate man.

Pontius Pilate – Cockney Rhyming Slang for 'toilet'.

Pony – Yes, it means a small horse, but also is slang for Twenty-Five pounds (money).

Pony-Up – To pay for something.

Pony and Trap – Cockney Rhyming Slang for 'crap'.

Poof – A homosexual.

Poontang – Sex.

Pooper Scooper – Small scoop to pick up dog's mess.

Poor Man's Gruel – Cockney Rhyming Slang for 'Liverpool'.

Pootle – Dawdle, walk unhurriedly.

Pop – Pawn.

Pope in Rome – Cockney Rhyming Slang for 'home'.

Pop Your Clogs – Basically this phrase means dying.

Pork & Cheese – Cockney Rhyming Slang for 'Portuguese'.

Porkies – Cockney Rhyming Slang for lies. "Porky pies", meaning "pork pies". Rhymes with lies. My Mum always used to tell me not to tell porkies!

Pork Pies – Cockney Rhyming Slang for 'lies'.

Pork Sword – Penis.

Porno Mag – Cockney Rhyming Slang for 'slag'.

Porridge - Doing porridge means to serve time in prison. There was also a comedy TV series called Porridge about a prisoner starring Ronnie Barker of The Two Ronnies fame.

Posh - High class. Comes from the cabins used by the upper class on early voyages from England to India. The coolest (and most expensive cabins) were Port side on the way Out and Starboard on the way Home.

Posh & Becks – Cockney Rhyming Slang for 'specs', glasses. Also 'sex'.

Poser – Show-off.

Postage Stamp – Cockney Rhyming Slang for 'tramp'.

Postie – The postman.

Postman Pat – Cockney Rhyming Slang for 'fat'. (origins; kids TV programme)

Pot & Pan – Cockney Rhyming Slang for 'old man', father.

Pot of Glue – Cockney Rhyming Slang for 'clue'.

Potatoes in the Mould – Cockney Rhyming Slang for 'cold'.

Pots & Dishes – Cockney Rhyming Slang for 'wishes'.

Potty - A little crazy, a bit of a looney, one card short of a full deck.

Potty-Mouthed – Swears a lot, foul-mouthed.

Pram – A baby carriage, short for 'perambulator'.

Pram-Face – A poor teenage mother, derogatory phrase.

Prang – To crash a car.

Prat – Stupid/annoying person.

PTO - This is an abbreviation for "please turn over". You will see it on forms in the UK where you would see the single word over in the USA.

Premium Bond – government issue lottery investment thing.

Prick – Penis, also an insult.

Prince's Trust – Cockney Rhyming Slang for 'bust', boobs.

Procurator Fiscal – Scottish, for chief public prosecutor.

Proper Job – A job well done, also top-class. "I bought a BMW last week, leather seats, proper job!"

Pub – Bar, drinking establishment.

Pub Crawl – Drinking trip, walking from one bar to the next etc etc.

Public Convenience – A Public Toilet.

Pudding – Desert. Basically anything you have as a desert… except ice cream… that's called ice cream.

Puff – Cannabis.

Puggled – Scottish slang for tired out.

Pukka - Super or smashing.

Pull – Looking for sex.

Pull a Fast One – To succeed in the art/game of deception. To play un unfair trick.

Pull a Sickie – To take a day off work, usually not being sick.

Pull Down The Shutter – Cockney Rhyming Slang for 'butter'.

Pull Someone's Plonker – To pull someone's leg, to joke.

Pull the Other One, (It's Got Bells On) – "I don't believe you'.

Pull Your Finger Out – Get working, get going.

Punch & Judy – Cockney Rhyming Slang for 'moody'.

Punch Up the Bracket – Punch in the face.

Punch in the Knickers – Good looking person.

Punnet – A small tray for holding strawberries.

Punter – A customer, a normal person who uses the facilities.

Push & Shove – Cockney Rhyming Slang for 'love'.

Push in the Truck – Cockney Rhyming Slang for 'f*ck'.

Push the Boat Out – Spend extravagantly.

Pussy – Vagina.

Pussy-Whipped – A man under his woman's control.

Put a Sock In It - This is one way of telling someone to shut up.

Put Away – Put in prison.

Put Paid to - To put an end to something. "Rain put paid to the cricket match."

Put the Wood in the Hole – Close the Door.

Q IS FOR QUANGO

Quack – Doctor.

QUANGO – Quasi-Autonomous non-Governmental organization. Think tank, derogatory.

Queen – Effeminate man.

Queen Mum – Cockney Rhyming Slang for 'bum'.

Queen of the Midden – Conceited woman.

Queens Park Ranger – Cockney Rhyming Slang for 'stranger'.

Queer – Looking ill, gay, strange.

Queer Street – Financial trouble.

Quentin Crisp – Cockney Rhyming Slang for 'lisp'.

Quentin Tarantino – Cockney Rhyming Slang for 'vino', wine.

Quid - A pound (money).

Quid's In – Being up on the deal.

Quine – Young girl (NE Scotland)

Quite - When used alone, this word means the same as absolutely!

R IS FOR RIGHT LITTLE EARNER

Rabbit – Talk. "She's got more Rabbit than Sainsbury's"; she talks a lot.

Rabbit & Pork – Cockney Rhyming Slang for 'talk'.

Rabbit Hutch – Cockney Rhyming Slang for 'clutch', 'crutch'.

Rabbit in a Hat – Cockney Rhyming Slang for 'twat', vagina.

Radge – Weird, strange, crazy, also good, great.

Radio Rental – Cockney Rhyming Slang for 'mental'.

Radio Transmitter – Cockney Rhyming Slang for 'shitter', arsehole.

Rag Week – A woman's menstrual period.

Rainbow Trout – Cockney Rhyming Slang for 'kraut', German.

Raining Cats and Dogs – Raining hard.

Raining Stair Rods – Really raining hard.

Rammed – Stuffed, completely full.

Randolph Scott – Cockney Rhyming Slang for 'spot'.

Rank – Crap, terrible, smelly, stinking.

Rant & Rave – Cockney Rhyming Slang for 'shave'.

Raquel Welch – Cockney Rhyming Slang for 'belch'.

Rare as Hen's Teeth – Very rare.

Raspberry Ripple – Cockney Rhyming Slang for 'nipple', 'cripple'.

Raspberry Tart – Cockney Rhyming Slang for 'fart', 'heart'.

Rasher of Bacon – One slice of bacon.

Raspberry – Cockney Rhyming Slang for a fart noise. Blowing 'raspberry tarts'.

Rat & Mouse – Cockney Rhyming Slang for 'house'.

Rat Arsed - Drunk, sloshed or plastered.

Rats & Mice – Cockney Rhyming Slang for 'dice'.

Rattle & Hum – Cockney Rhyming Slang for 'come'.

Ravi Shankar – Cockney Rhyming Slang for 'wanker'.

Ray Mears – Cockney Rhyming Slang for 'beers'.

Razor – Cockney Rhyming Slang for 'blazer'.

Read - Your major at school. "What did you read at Oxford?"

Readies – Cash money.

Real McCoy – Real, genuine, not faked.

Real Madrid – Cockney Rhyming Slang for 'quid', pound.

Reccy – A quick initial look; from 'reconnaissance'.

Red 'n' Yella – Cockney Rhyming Slang for 'umbrella'.

Red Red Rubies – Cockney Rhyming Slang for 'boobies'.

Red Rose – Cockney Rhyming Slang for 'nose'.

Redundancy - If you are made redundant it means you are laid off.

Reels of Cotton – Cockney Rhyming Slang for 'rotten'.

Reg Varney – Cockney Rhyming Slang for 'sarnie', sandwich, also 'Pakistani'. (origins; comedian)

Reggie Blinker – Cockney Rhyming Slang for 'stinker', bad game.

Rellie – Liverpool for 'relative'.

Remembrance Day – Armistice Day, 11th November.

Rent Boy - Rale prostitute.

Reverse the Charges – Call Collect. When you want to ring someone up and you have no money you can call the operator and ask to reverse the charges in the UK.

Rex Mossop – Cockney Rhyming Slang for 'gossip'.

Rhubarb Crumble – Cockney Rhyming Slang for 'grumble'.

Rhubarb Hill – Cockney Rhyming Slang for 'pill'.

Rhythm & Blues – Cockney Rhyming Slang for 'shoes'.

Ribena – Blackcurrant drink, to be diluted with water, or lemonade.

Riccardo Patrese – Cockney Rhyming Slang for 'hazy'.

Richard & Judy – Cockney Rhyming Slang for 'moody'.

Richard Burtons – Cockney Rhyming Slang for 'curtains'.

Richard Gere – Cockney Rhyming Slang for 'beer'.

Richard the Third – Cockney Rhyming Slang for 'bird', 'turd'.

Rick Whitter – Cockney Rhyming Slang for 'shitter', arsehole.

Ricky Lake – Cockney Rhyming Slang for 'fake'.

Ricky & Bianca – Cockney Rhyming Slang for 'wanker'.

Ricky Gervais – Cockney Rhyming Slang for 'face'.

Riddick Bowe – Cockney Rhyming Slang for 'B.O.', body odour.

Rifle Range – Cockney Rhyming Slang for 'change', coins.

Right as Ninepence – Very good.

Right – Very. "I'm feeling right knackered."

Right Charlie – Looking the fool.

Right Little Earner – Job that pays good money.

Right On – Cool, good, great.

Right One – A stand out character, but not in a good way.

Right Said Fred – Cockney Rhyming Slang for 'dead', 'bread'.

Ring – To call someone on the phone "I'll give you a ring tomorrow."

Ringer – Stolen car changed to appear legitimate.

Rigobert Song – Cockney Rhyming Slang for 'thong'.

Ringo Starr – Cockney Rhyming Slang for 'bar'.

Ring Road – Traffic assistance road round a town, detour.

Ring Stinger – A very hot curry.

Rink a Dink – Cockney Rhyming Slang for 'chink', Chinese.

Rio Ferdinand – Cockney Rhyming Slang for 'grand', a thousand pounds. (origins; footballer) – 2nd Degree Cockney Rhyming Slang "That just cost me a Rio".

Rip Off – Defraud, sell counterfeit, a deal leaving you out of pocket.

River Nile – Cockney Rhyming Slang for 'denial'.

River Ouse – Cockney Rhyming Slang for 'booze'.

Roach – A drug joint.

Roast Pork – Cockney Rhyming Slang for 'fork'.

Roasty – Roast potato, or a roast beef dinner.

Roath – Four.

Rob Roy – Cockney Rhyming Slang for 'boy'.

Robin Hood – Cockney Rhyming Slang for 'good'.

Robinson & Cleaver – Cockney Rhyming Slang for 'fever'.

Robinson Crusoe – Cockney Rhyming Slang for 'do so'.

Rock & Roll – Cockney Rhyming Slang for 'doll', unemployment benefit.

Rocking – very good, great, excellent.

Rock of Ages – Cockney Rhyming Slang for 'wages'.

Rocking Horse – Cockney Rhyming Slang for 'sauce'.

Roger - To have sex with, from a male perspective.

Roger Mellie – Cockney Rhyming Slang for 'telly', television.

Roger Moore – Cockney Rhyming Slang for 'door'.

Roger Starling – Cockney Rhyming Slang for 'Carling', Black label, lager.

Roland Rat – Cockney Rhyming Slang for 'twat'. (origins; kids cartoon)

Roller Coaster – Cockney Rhyming Slang for 'toaster', 'poster'.

Rolls Royce – Cockney Rhyming Slang for 'choice'.

Rolly – Home rolled cigarette.

Roman Candles – Cockney Rhyming Slang for 'sandals'.

Ronald de Boer – Cockney Rhyming Slang for 'score'.

Ronald Riches – Cockney Rhyming Slang for 'bitches'.

Ronan Keating – Cockney Rhyming Slang for 'cheating', 'meeting''. (origins; singer)

Ronnie Barker – Cockney Rhyming Slang for 'marker', pen.

Ronnie Corbett – Cockney Rhyming Slang for 'orbit'.

Ronson Lighter – Cockney Rhyming Slang for 'shiter', toilet.

Roof Rack – Cockney Rhyming Slang for 'back'.

Roof Tile – Cockney Rhyming Slang for 'smile'.

Rory McGrath – Cockney Rhyming Slang for 'laugh'. (origins; comedian)

Rory O'Moore – Cockney Rhyming Slang for 'door', 'floor'.

Rosie Lea – Cockney Rhyming Slang for 'tea'. The drink.

Rough as a Badgers Arse – Very rough, usually ugly, not good looking.

Rouf Cinque – 45 degrees.

Round - A drink for everyone in your group in a bar. "Hey, Jimmy, don't leave now, it's your round."

Round the Houses – Cockney Rhyming Slang for 'trousers'.

Row - (rhyming with 'cow') An argument.

Royal Navy – Cockney Rhyming Slang for 'gravy'.

Roy Hudd's – Cockney Rhyming Slang for 'blood', 'spud'. (origins; comedian)

Rozzer – Policeman.

Rub a Dub – Cockney Rhyming Slang for 'pub', 'sub'.

Rubber Duck – Cockney Rhyming Slang for 'f*ck'.

Rubber Glove – Cockney Rhyming Slang for 'love'.

Rubber Gregory – Cockney Rhyming Slang for 'bouncing cheque/check', from Gregory Peck-check.

Rubber Johnny – Condom.

Rubbish - Trash or garbage. You might also accuse someone of talking rubbish.

Rubik's Cube – Cockney Rhyming Slang for 'tube, 'pube'.

Ruby Murray – Cockney Rhyming Slang for 'curry'. Ruby was an Irish singer of the 40's.

Ruck – A rugby term for men, in a pile, fighting for the ball. Also used as a fight or rumpus.

Rug – Wig.

Rug Rats – Children, toddlers.

Rug Muncher – Lesbian.

Rugger - Another name for "rugby".

Rum & Coke – Cockney Rhyming Slang for 'joke'.

Rumbled – Caught, caught out, discovered.

Rum Do – A strange situation or event.

Rumpy Pumpy – Sex, hanky panky, or a bit of nookie!

Runner Bean – Cockney Rhyming Slang for 'queen'.

Running Around Like a Blue-Arsed Fly – Slang for 'being really busy', with the undercurrent of not getting much done.

Runs, The - Slang for 'diarrhea'.

Russell Crowe – Cockney Rhyming Slang for 'dough', money.

Russell Harty – Cockney Rhyming Slang for 'party'.

Rusty Bucket – Cockney Rhyming Slang for 'f*ck it'.

Rusty Lee – Cockney Rhyming Slang for 'pee', 'wee'.

Rusty Nail – Cockney Rhyming Slang for 'jail'.

Rusty Spike – Cockney Rhyming Slang for 'dyke', lesbian.

Ruud Hullit – Cockney Rhyming Slang for 'gullet'.

S IS FOR SANDY LYLE

Sack/sacked - If someone gets 'the sack' it means they are fired. They have been sacked. I can think of a few people I'd like to sack!

Sad - Naff, stupid, uncool or unfashionable. "You sad bastard".

Saddam Hussein – Cockney Rhyming Slang for 'insane'.

Safe – Good, okay.

Sage & Onion – Cockney Rhyming Slang for 'bunion'.

Salad Dodger – Fat person.

Salvadore Dali – Cockney Rhyming Slang for 'charlie', cocaine.

Salford Docks – Cockney Rhyming Slang for 'rocks'.

Salmon & Trout – Cockney Rhyming Slang for 'snout', 'grout', 'stout'.

Salt Lake City – Cockney Rhyming Slang for 'titty', breast.

Salvation Army – Cockney Rhyming Slang for 'barmy'.

Samantha Mumba – Cockney Rhyming Slang for 'number'.

Samba Brazilian – Cockney Rhyming Slang for 'civilian'.

San Bruno – Cockney Rhyming Slang for 'pruno', prison alcohol.

Sandwich Short of a Picnic – Stupid, backward, mentally challenged.

Sandy Lyle – Cockney Rhyming Slang for 'style', 'smile'. (origins; golfer)

Sandy McNabs – Cockney Rhyming Slang for 'crabs, STD.

Santas Grotto – Cockney Rhyming Slang for 'blotto', drunk.

San Toy – Cockney Rhyming Slang for 'toy'.

Sapper – Army talk for engineer.

Sara Cox – Cockney Rhyming Slang for 'socks'.

Sarky – Short for 'Sarcastic'. "Don't you get sarky with me, young man!"

Sarnie – Sandwich.

Sassenach – Scottish term for Englishman, born south of the border, lowlander.

Saucepan Handle – Cockney Rhyming Slang for 'candle'.

Saucepan Lid – Cockney Rhyming Slang for 'kid', 'quid', pound.

Sausage & Mash – Cockney Rhyming Slang for 'slash', pee, 'cash', 'crash'.

Sausage Roll – Cockney Rhyming Slang for 'doll', welfare, 'goal'.

Sausage Sarnie – Cockney Rhyming Slang for 'Pakistani'.

Saville Row – A street in London famous for upmarket men's clothes, suits etc.

Scally – Short for scallywag, ruffian.

Scanties – Underwear, usually thin, almost irrelevant.

Scapa Flow – Cockney Rhyming Slang for 'go'.

Scarper – Second degree Cockney Rhyming Slang for 'run away'. Scapa Flow; harbor in the Shetlands where the WW1 German fleet was scuttled.

Schindler's List – Cockney Rhyming Slang for 'pissed', 'wrist'.

Schtum – Usually 'Keeping Schtum', means keeping quiet about something/a secret. Keeping your mouth shut.

Scooby Doo – Second degree Cockney Rhyming Slang for 'clue'. "He's not got a Scooby!"

Scooby Doos – Cockney Rhyming Slang for 'shoes'.

Scoor-oot – Scottish; Throwing of change at a wedding (short for scatter-out)

Score – Twenty.

Scotch Egg – Boiled egg, surrounded by meatloaf, then breadcrumbs.

Scotch Eggs – Cockney Rhyming Slang for 'legs'.

Scotch Mist – Cockney Rhyming Slang for 'pissed', drunk.

Scotch Mist – Nothing.

Scouser – Someone from Liverpool.

Scramble – The throwing of change (cash) at a wedding. ("Scoor-oot" in Scotland short for scatter-out)

Scran – Food.

Scratch 'n' Sniff – Cockney Rhyming Slang for 'spliff'.

Scratcher – Slang for your bed, where you sleep.

Scratch Yer Head – Cockney Rhyming Slang for 'bed'.

Screaming Abdabs – Fear, having the jitters.

Screaming Blue Murder – Shout, scream, be angry or mad.

Screaming Alice – Cockney Rhyming Slang for 'Crystal Palace'.

Screaming Lord Such – Cockney Rhyming Slang for 'crutch'.

Screw – Have sex with.

Screw Loose – To be slightly mad, insane, not right in the head.

Scrote – Criminal, a bad or annoying person. Probably from 'scrotum'.

Scrub Up Well – Dressed up/washed for an occasion, or to go out.

Scrummy – Scrumptious, delicious.

Scrumpy – Home-made (farm-made, not commercially made) apple cider.

Scrumping - To go stealing - usually apples from someone elses trees!

Scunner – An expression of surprise, to flummox.

Sean Bean – Cockney Rhyming Slang for 'mean'.

Sean Ryder – Cockney Rhyming Slang for 'cyder'.

Sebastian Coes – Cockney Rhyming Slang for 'toes'. (origins; athlete)

Sebs – Shortened term of above.

Secateurs – Rose cutters. (sick-at-ears)

Second Hand Merc – Cockney Rhyming Slang for 'Turk'.

Secondary School – High School.

Second Year Student – A student in their second year at a school/college/university.

See a Man About a Dog – To go to the toilet.

See You Anon – See you later, goodbye.

Selina Scott – Cockney Rhyming Slang for 'spot'.

Semi – A partial erection.

Semi-Detached – A duplex house. Two houses attached to one another.

Sen – Yorkshire for yourself.

Send-up - To send someone up is to make fun of them.

Sent Down – Sent to prison, convicted.

Sent To Coventry – Purposefully ignored in a mass/big way.

Septic Tank – Cockney Rhyming Slang for 'wank'.

Septic Tank – Cockney Rhyming Slang for 'Yank'.

Serviette – Napkin.

Sexton Blake – Cockney Rhyming Slang for 'steak'. 'cake', 'fake'.

Shabba Ranks – Cockney Rhyming Slang for 'thanks'.

Shag - To have sex with.

Shagged - Past tense of shag, but also see knackered.

Shake & Shiver – Cockney Rhyming Slang for 'river'.

Shaken Not Stirred – Cockney Rhyming Slang for 'bird'.

Shakin Stevens – Cockney Rhyming Slang for 'evens'.

Shambles – Chaotic, a real mess. Also an old name for a slaughterhouse.

Shambolic (In a Shambles) - In a state of chaos.

Shandy – Beer or lager mixed with 7up or Sprite.

Shank – To stab, usually with a knife, or home made weapon, (in prison).

Shank's Pony – A phrase which means to 'have to walk'. I'm thinking that at some point, Mr. Shanks didn't have a pony.

Sharking – To drink other people's unfinished drinks.

Sharon Stone – Cockney Rhyming Slang for 'phone'.

Shawshank Redemption – Cockney Rhyming Slang for 'pension'.

Shebang – The whole thing.

Shed Load – A whole lot of whatever you're talking about.

Sheffield United – Cockney Rhyming Slang for 'excited'.

Shell Out – Pay for. Lay out money for.

Shell Suit – Weird thin material track-suit from the eighties.

Shepherd's Pie – Meat & Vegetable casserole dish (traditionally minced lamb) with mashed potatoes on top.

Shepherd's Plaid – Cockney Rhyming Slang for 'bad'.

Sherbet Dab – Cockney Rhyming Slang for 'cab'.

Sherbet Dip – Cockney Rhyming Slang for 'kip', sleep.

Shereen Nanjiani – Cockney Rhyming Slang for 'fanny', vagina.

Sherman Tank – Cockney Rhyming Slang for 'wank', masturbate.

Shetland Isles – Cockney Rhyming Slang for 'piles', hemorrhoids.

Shift – To move, or to move something. Also slang for a days work.

Shilling Short of a Pound - Stupid, backward, mentally challenged.

Shine a Light – slang for saying 'shite'.

Shiner – Black eye.

Ship Full Sail – Cockney Rhyming Slang for 'pint of ale'.

Ship's Anchor – Cockney Rhyming Slang for 'wanker'.

Shipshape and Bristol Fashion – Everything is in order.

Shirley Basset – Cockney Rhyming Slang for 'chassis'.

Shirt Front – Cockney Rhyming Slang for 'c*nt'.

Shirty – To mouth off, to backchat. "Don't get shirty with me young man"

Shite – Another word for 'shit'.

Shites – Slang for diarrhea.

Shitfaced - Steaming drunk.

Shit For Brains – An idiot, fool.

Shit in a Hurry – Cockney Rhyming Slang for 'curry'.

Shite Hawk – Liar.

Shitter – Used both for anus and toilet.

Shitting Bricks – Very frightened, terrified.

Shoddy – Poor quality, bad workmanship.

Shoe-In – A certainty.

Shoot the Crow (Craw) – Scottish slang for going away, leaving.

Shop Front – Cockney Rhyming Slang for 'c*nt'.

Short and Curlies – Pubic hair.

Short & Stout – Cockney Rhyming Slang for 'Kraut', German.

Shovel & Pick – Cockney Rhyming Slang for 'nick', prison.

Shovel & Spade – Cockney Rhyming Slang for 'blade', knife.

Shove Off – Get lost, also when your boat leaves the wharf.

Shrapnel – Loose change, coin money.

Shredded Wheat - Cockney Rhyming Slang for 'cheat'.

Shreddies – Underpants.

Shufti (Shifty) - Pronounced shooftee; to take a look at something, to take a butchers!

Shut Your Cakehole – Shut up.

Shut Your Gob – Shut up.

Shyster – A conman, trickster, man of dubious morals.

Sick – Good, great.

Sick as a Parrot – Pretty badly sick.

Sick to the Back Teeth – Fed up with something, had enough.

Side – A snooker term for a swerve shot, called "English" in USA.

Sieg Heils – Cockney Rhyming Slang for 'piles', hemorrhoids.

Sigourney Weaver – Cockney Rhyming Slang for 'beaver'.

Silly Buggers – Horsing around, not taking things seriously "He was always playing silly buggers".

Silly Season – A time of the week, month, year when the silly, unexpected makes the news.

Silvery Moon – Cockney Rhyming Slang for 'coon', black person.

Silvery Spoon – Cockney Rhyming Slang for 'coon', black person.

Sim – A simpleton, backward, mentally challenged.

Simon Cowell – Cockney Rhyming Slang for 'trowel'.

Simon Schamas – Cockney Rhyming Slang for 'pyjamas'.

Simples (Simps) – An easy task, simple.

Sinbad the Sailor – Cockney Rhyming Slang for 'tailor'.

Sir Arthur Bliss – Cockney Rhyming Slang for 'piss', pee.

Sistine Chapel – Cockney Rhyming Slang for 'apple'.

Six & Eight – Cockney Rhyming Slang for 'state', condition.

Sixes and Sevens - In a mess, topsy-turvy, somewhat haywire!

Skater Hater – A person who hates skaters, skateboarders.

Skein of Thread – Cockney Rhyming Slang for 'bed'.

Skelf – Scottish for splinter.

Skelp – To slap someone.

Skew-Whiff – Crooked, not level, not right.

Skin & Blister – Cockney Rhyming Slang for 'sister'.

Skinful – A whole lot of alcohol consumed, usually can't take any more.

Skint – Broke, no money.

Skip – Avoid, play truant, skive.

Skive - To evade something. (Like skipping school).

Skiver – Someone who's evading something. Being lazy. Getting out of doing work.

Skivvy – Underwear, or a person who does dirty jobs. "The doctor told me to strip down to my skivvies".

Skoosh – juice, pop, lemonade.

Skunk – Cannabis weed.

Sky Diver – Cockney Rhyming Slang for 'fiver', five pounds.

Sky Rocket – Cockney Rhyming Slang for 'pocket'.

Slag - To bad mouth someone, also a girl who sleeps around.

Slainte – Scottish greeting, pronounced 'slanje'. Means good health, A Scottish toast said over whisky.

Slamming – Attractive, good-looking.

Slander & Libel – Cockney Rhyming Slang for 'Bible'.

Slap – Make-up, face cream.

Slap-Head – Bald person.

Slap Up Meal – A really good meal, usually meaning it cost a fair bit.

Slap and Tickle – Slang for having sex.

Slapper - A female who is a bit loose, a slag or a tart.

Slash – Urination. To pee.

Slattering – Raining hard.

Slay 'em in the Ailes – Cockney Rhyming Slang for 'piles', hemorrhoids.

Sleeping Policeman - An expression for Speedbump.

Slice Pan – Cockney Rhyming Slang for 'van'. (origins; type of bread)

Sling Your Hook – Leaving. Getting out of somewhere.

Slip Her a Length – Sex, providing the female with a 'length' of something she wants.

Slippery Slope – Cockney Rhyming Slang for 'dope'.

Slits in a Dress – Cockney Rhyming Slang for 'mess'.

Slog Your Guts Out – Working really, really hard.

Sloshed - Drunk.

Slut-Shaming – To bully someone into admitting they sleep around.

Smack – Heroin.

Smackers – Paper money, pounds.

Small Geezers – Cockney Rhyming Slang for 'Maltesers'. (origins; confection)

Small Potatoes – The small stuff in life. The minutiae.

Smarmy – Smooth talker, someone who has a way with the ladies.

Smarties – Sweets, like M&M's.

Smash & Grab – Cockney Rhyming Slang for 'cab'.

Smash & Grab – quick robbery.

Smashing - If something is smashing, it means it is terrific.

Smeg – Derogatory term from 'Red Dwarf'. The dictionary definition says it is a "sebaceous secretion from under the foreskin".

Smidgeon – A little bit, not a lot, a dab.

Smirr – Scottish for drizzle, raining slightly, wet and misty.

Smoke Screen – Cockney Rhyming Slang for 'Queen'.

Smooth as a Baby's Bottom – very smooth indeed.

Snake's Hiss – Cockney Rhyming Slang for 'piss', 'kiss'.

Snatch – Vagina.

Snazzy – Looking good, well dressed.

Snitch – To 'grass' on someone, to turn someone in, give information to the police to get someone arrested.

Snog - To make out, kiss.

Snookered – In a bad or tricky situation. Up the famous creek without a paddle. From the game of snooker where you are unable to hit the ball because the shot is blocked by your opponent's ball.

Snout – Rolling tobacco.

Snow & Slush – Cockney Rhyming Slang for 'flush', have money.

So and So – General derogatory term. "He's a nosey so-and-so".

Sock & Blister – Cockney Rhyming Slang for 'sister'.

Sod – Another general derogatory term.

Sod All – Nothing.

Sod Off – Means 'get lost' or a polite way of saying 'f*ck off'.

Sod's Law - This is another name for Murphy's law - whatever can go wrong, will go wrong.

Sod That For a Game of Soldiers – "I'm not doing that".

Sofa Surfing – Living on someone's couch temporarily.

Soft in the Head - A simpleton, backward, mentally challenged.

Sol Campbell – Cockney Rhyming Slang for 'ramble', 'gamble'. (origins; footballer)

Son & Daughtered – Cockney Rhyming Slang for 'slaughtered'.

Song and Dance – To be upset, cause a scene, "It's only a broken cup, no need to make a song and dance about it!"

Sonny Jim – General affectionate term.

Sooty & Sweep – Cockney Rhyming Slang for 'sleep'. (origins; puppets)

Soppy – Lovey-dovey, affectionate.

Sorry & Sad – Cockney Rhyming Slang for 'bad'.

Sorted - Arranged, organized, satisfied, content.

Soup & Gravy – Cockney Rhyming Slang for 'Navy'.

Soused – Drunk.

Southpaw – Left-handed.

Sov – One pound (short for sovereign)

Sozzled – Drunk.

Space Hopper – Cockney Rhyming Slang for 'copper', police.

Spanish Onion – Cockney Rhyming Slang for 'bunion'.

Spanish Waiter – Cockney Rhyming Slang for 'potato', (potater), also 'see ya later'.

Spanner – Wrench, adjustable wrench, also a stupid person.

Spanner in the Works – A problem, also to sabotage.

Spark Plugs – Cockney Rhyming Slang for 'drugs'.

Spark/Sparky – Electrician.

Speckled Hen – Cockney Rhyming Slang for 'ten', usually pounds.

Specky Four-Eyes – Wearing glasses, specs.

Speciality - Specialty with an extra 'i'.

Spend a Penny - Go to the bathroom. In olden times, public toilets had a penny slot.

Spiders & Bugs – Cockney Rhyming Slang for 'thugs'.

Spider's Web – Cockney Rhyming Slang for 'pleb'.

Spiffing – Good, excellent.

Spit & a Drag – Cockney Rhyming Slang for 'fag', cigarette.

Spliff – A joint.

Spiv – Con-man, person of questionable morals.

Splash Out - Spend far too much money.

Spondulicks – Great, wonderful.

Sportsman's Bet – Cockney Rhyming Slang for 'Internet'.

Spotted Dick – Cake with raisins in.

Spotty Dog – Cockney Rhyming Slang for 'bog', toilet.

Sprog – Child, toddler.

Sprinkle – To pee, urinate.

Spuds – Potatoes.

Spurtle – Scottish slang for wooden spoon.

Square Go – A fight, to fight.

Squeeze – Boyfriend or girlfriend.

Squid – Cockney Rhyming Slang for 'quid', pound.

Squiddly Did – Cockney Rhyming Slang for 'quid', pound.

Squidgy – Spongey, soft.

Squiffy - Feeling a little drunk, also 'gone wrong'.

Squire – Term of address to a male stranger.

Squits – Diarrhoea.

Sri Lanker – Cockney Rhyming Slang for 'wanker'.

St Louis Blues – Cockney Rhyming Slang for 'shoes'.

St Martins-le-Grand – Cockney Rhyming Slang for 'hand'.

Stacked – To be rich, also large breasts.

Stag Night – Batchelor party (men).

Stamford Bridge – Cockney Rhyming Slang for 'fridge'.

Stammer & Stutter – Cockney Rhyming Slang for 'butter'.

Stand at Ease – Cockney Rhyming Slang for 'cheese'.

Starkers - No clothes on, naked.

Stars & Garters – Cockney Rhyming Slang for 'tomatoes', (tomarters).

Star's Nap – Cockney Rhyming Slang for 'tap', borrow. "Can I tap you for a fiver 'til Monday?"

Starsky & Hutch – Cockney Rhyming Slang for 'clutch'.

Steak & Kidney Pie – Cockney Rhyming Slang for 'fly'.

Steam Tug – Cockney Rhyming Slang for 'mug'.

Steaming – Really drunk.

Steely Dan – Cockney Rhyming Slang for 'tan'.

Steffi Graf – Cockney Rhyming Slang for 'laugh'.

Steve Claridge – Cockney Rhyming Slang for 'garage'. (origins; footballer)

Steve McQueens – Cockney Rhyming Slang for 'jeans'.

Stevey Bold – Cockney Rhyming Slang for 'cold'.

Stevie Nicks – Cockney Rhyming Slang for 'flicks', pictures, cinema.

Stevie Wonder – Cockney Rhyming Slang for 'chunder', be sick, throw up.

Stewart Granger – Cockney Rhyming Slang for 'danger'. "Any Stewart (danger, chance) of getting that fiver back?"

Stewed Prune – Cockney Rhyming Slang for 'tune'.

Stick of Glue – Cockney Rhyming Slang for 'Jew'.

Stick One on Someone – Punch someone.

Sticks & Stones – Cockney Rhyming Slang for 'bones'.

Stick Your Neck Out – Go on a hunch. Be brave, brazen.

Sticky Toffee – Cockney Rhyming Slang for 'coffee'.

Sticky Wicket – Difficult or tricky situation.

Stiffy - Another word for erection.

Stinging Nettle – Cockney Rhyming Slang for 'kettle'.

Stirling Moss – Cockney Rhyming Slang for 'toss'. (origins; racing driver) "I **don't give a toss, mate".** = "I don't care much".

Stitch That – Expression usually said after hitting someone.

Stitch Up – A contrived situation, a pre-planned result.

Stoater – Scottish for great, good, beauty.

Stock Market Crash – Cockney Rhyming Slang for 'slash'.

Stoked – Happy, chuffed, delighted.

Stoke on Trent – Cockney Rhyming Slang for 'bent', homosexual.

Stone the Crows (Stone Me) – general exclamation of surprise; same as 'cor blimey' or 'blow me down'.

Stonker (Stonking) – Huge, oversized.

Stookie - Scottish for a plaster cast on a broken bone. Also Scottish for standing around uselessly immobile. "Standin' aroon' like a stookie!"

Stop Thief – Cockney Rhyming Slang for 'beef'.

Stowed out – Busy beyond room. Really busy with no room to move.

Stramash – Scottish slang for a great party, or a bit of bother, trouble, a fight (or all together).

Strange & Weird – Cockney Rhyming Slang for 'beard'.

Strapped – Broke, no money.

Strawberry Split – Cockney Rhyming Slang for 'twit', 'git'.

Strawberry Tart – Cockney Rhyming Slang for 'heart'.

Street Fighter – Cockney Rhyming Slang for 'lighter'.

Stretch – Time in prison, a prison sentence.

Strewth – A general exclamation of surprise; same as 'cor blimey' or 'blow me down'.

Strides – Trousers.

String of Beads – Cockney Rhyming Slang for 'Leeds'.

Strike a Light – A general exclamation of surprise; same as 'cor blimey' or 'blow me down'.

Stroppy – Shirty, mouthy, cheeky.

Stuff It - An expression of dismissal. "To hell with it, I'm going home!"

Struggle & Grunt – Cockney Rhyming Slang for 'c*nt'.

Stump Up – To pay for something.

Stunting – Showing off.

Sue Lawley – Cockney Rhyming Slang for 'poorly', ill. (origins; newsreader)

Sugar Candy – Cockney Rhyming Slang for 'handy'.

Sultana – A juicy raisin. Golden raisin.

Summat – Yorkshire slang for 'Something'.

Sunday Roast – Cockney Rhyming Slang for 'post'.

Sunny Dancer – Cockney Rhyming Slang for 'cancer'.

Supersonic – Cockney Rhyming Slang for 'Gin & Tonic'.

Surrey Docks – Cockney Rhyming Slang for 'pox'.

Suss - Figured out. Figure out. "He said it was a secret, but I soon sussed it out".

Swanee River – Cockney Rhyming Slang for 'liver'.

Sweater Muffins – Woman's breasts.

Sweaty Sock – Cockney Rhyming Slang for 'Jock', Scotsman.

Sweeney Todd – Cockney Rhyming Slang for the 'flying squad', police.

Sweet Fanny Adams - Nothing or sod all. It is a polite substitute for 'sweet f**k all', also shortened further to 'Sweet F A'.

Swings and Roundabouts – Comparing two things that are either close or far apart physically.

Swiss Roll – Cockney Rhyming Slang for 'Pole', Polish person.

Swotting – To study hard, cram for an exam.

Syrup of Figs – Cockney Rhyming Slang for 'wig'. "Oh, look at the syrup he's wearing!"

T IS FOR TOM, DICK & HARRY

TA – Territorial Army (Army Reserve)

T & H – Eight.

Ta - Short for thanks.

Tab Hanging – Listening in, overhearing.

Tackle – The male sexual organs.

Tad – A little bit. "I'll have a tad of butter on my potatoes."

Tadger – Penis.

Taff (Taffy) – Slang for Welshman.

Take a Running Jump – Phrase for "Get Lost".

Takeaway – Carry-out.

Taking the Biscuit - Out-does everything else and cannot be bettered.

Taking the Mick (Mickey) - See next entry. Variations include "taking the mick", "extracting the Michael".

Taking the Piss - Make fun of someone.

Talent - Talent is the same as totty. Checking out the talent means looking for the sexy young girls (or boys I suppose).

Talk & Mutter – Cockney Rhyming Slang for 'butter'.

Talk Out of One's Arse – Talk shite, talk rubbish, no facts or substance.

Talk the Hind legs Off a Donkey – One person talking WAY too much, for WAY too long.

Tammy – Tampon.

Tangoed – Slapped on the ears with both hands. (From an old orange juice commercial)

Tanner – Sixpence, (old money).

Tannoy System – The Public Address system.

Tara - Pronounced "churar", this is another word for cheerio or goodbye.

Tart – Loose woman.

Tartan Banner – Cockney Rhyming Slang for 'tanner', sixpence.

Tart Up – Dress up.

Tate & Lyles – Cockney Rhyming Slang for 'piles', hemorrhoids.

Taters in the Mould – Cockney Rhyming Slang for 'cold'.

Tatties – Scottish for potatoes.

Tea Caddy – Cockney Rhyming Slang for 'Paddy', Irishman.

Tea Leaf - Cockney Rhyming Slang for 'thief'.

Tea Leafing – Cockney Rhyming Slang for 'thieving'.

Tea Pot Lid – Cockney Rhyming Slang for 'Yid', Jew.

Tea, Two and a Bloater – Cockney Rhyming Slang for 'motor', car.

Teapot Lid – Cockney Rhyming Slang for 'kid', 'quid', pound.

Tear in a Bucket – Cockney Rhyming Slang for 'f*ck it'.

Technicolour Yawn – Vomit, be sick.

Ted Heath – Cockney Rhyming Slang for 'teeth'. (origins; Prime Minister)

Ted Ray – Cockney Rhyming Slang for 'gay', homosexual.

Teddington Lock – Cockney Rhyming Slang for 'sock'.

Telly – Television.

Ten Bob – Ten shillings old money, or 50p new money.

Ten Furlongs Mile & a Quarter – Cockney Rhyming Slang for 'water'.

Ten Ounce Rump – Cockney Rhyming Slang for 'dump, a defecation.

Ten Pinter – Ugly person, (who would look better after you've had ten pints of beer).

Ten Speed Gears – Cockney Rhyming Slang for 'ears'.

Tenner – Ten pound note.

Tennis Racquet – Cockney Rhyming Slang for 'jacket'.

Terrace Anthem – The songs at a football match.

Terry Butcher – Cockney Rhyming Slang for 'tail toucher, homosexual'. (origins; footballer)

Teuchter – Someone from the country. (Scottish)

Tex Ritter – Cockney Rhyming Slang for 'bitter', beer.

TFFT – "Thank f*ck for that".

That Takes the Biscuit – "That takes first prize", "Well, that takes the biscuit, he finished first, but lost his shoe halfway round!"

That's a Turn Up For the Books – An expression which means "That was unexpected."

The Full Monty – Everything.

Thelonious Monk – Cockney Rhyming Slang for 'spunk', sperm.

The Pits – The worst.

The Smoke – Town, also London.

Thick & Thin – Cockney Rhyming Slang for 'skin'.

Thick as a Brick – Slang for dumb, unintelligent, stupid.

Thick as a Plank – Slang for dumb, unintelligent, stupid.

Thick as Shite – Slang for dumb, unintelligent, stupid.

Thicko – Slang for dumb, unintelligent, stupid.

Thingamajig – A made up name for something which has no name or the name is forgotten.

Thingy – The name you substitute when you've forgotten its/his/her name.

Thirteen Amp – Cockney Rhyming Slang for 'tramp'.

This & That – Cockney Rhyming Slang for 'cat'.

Thomas Edison – Cockney Rhyming Slang for 'medicine'.

Thomas Moore – Cockney Rhyming Slang for 'whore'.

Thomas Tank – Cockney Rhyming Slang for 'wank', masturbate.

Thomas Tilling – Cockney Rhyming Slang for 'shilling'.

Thora Hird – Cockney Rhyming Slang for 'turd', shite.

Three Card Trick – Cockney Rhyming Slang for 'dick', penis.

Three Sheets to the Wind – Pretty drunk.

Three Wheel Trike – Cockney Rhyming Slang for 'dyke', lesbian.

Throw a Spanner in the Works - An expression which means to wreck/sabotage something.

Throw a Wobbler (Wobbly) – Get angry, be upset.

Throw Your Toys Out of the Pram – Loose your temper, childishly.

Thruppenny Bits – Yes, it is a pre-decimal coin with a value of three pence, but it's also Cockney Rhyming Slang for 'Tits'. Ladies mammary glands.

Thunder Thighs – A person with large thighs.

Tia Maria – Cockney Rhyming Slang for 'diarrhea'.

Tick – A small increment of time. "I'll be with you in a tick."

Tick Tock – Cockney Rhyming Slang for 'clock', 'knock'.

Ticket to the Dance – Cockney Rhyming Slang for 'redundance'.

Tickety-Boo - If something is going well with no problems we would say it is tickety-boo.

Tiddly – Slightly drunk

Tiddly Wink – Cockney Rhyming Slang for 'chink', Chinese food, also 'drink'.

Tide Someone Over – To make do until next time.

Tidy - Attractive or sexy.

Tight – Mean with money, also drunk.

Tight as a Duck's Arse – Mean with money.

Tightwad – Mean with money.

Tiffin – Lunchtime snack.

Tijuana Brass – Cockney Rhyming Slang for 'arse'.

Tilbury Docks – Cockney Rhyming Slang for 'socks'.

Tin Bath – Cockney Rhyming Slang for 'laugh'.

Tin Lids – Cockney Rhyming Slang for 'kids'.

Tin Roof – Cockney Rhyming Slang for 'poof', homosexual.

Tin Tack – Cockney Rhyming Slang for 'sack', paid off.

Tin Tank – Cockney Rhyming Slang for 'bank'.

Tinkle – Urinate, pee.

Tipping the Velvet – Cunnilingus, oral sex.

Tipsy – Mildly drunk.

Titfer – Short for 'tit for tat'.

Tit for Tat - Giving as good as getting, one turn deserves another.

Tit For Tat – Cockney Rhyming Slang for 'hat'.

Tits Up – Something gone wrong.

Tit Widow – Having no or very small breasts.

Tit Willow – Cockney Rhyming Slang for 'pillow'.

Toad in the Hole – Egg based dish with Tomato, sausage, grilled.

Toblerone – Cockney Rhyming Slang for 'alone', 'on my own'. (origins; confectionery)

To Boot – Also. "Not only did he run well, he won to boot".

Toby Rail – Cockney Rhyming Slang for 'ale'.

Toby Jug – Cockney Rhyming Slang for 'mug', face, also 'lug', ear.

Todd Carty – Cockney Rhyming Slang for 'party'.

Todd Sloane – Cockney Rhyming Slang for 'alone'.

Todger - Penis.

Toe Rag – General insult, meaning you're a bad or untrustworthy person.

Toe Rag – Cockney Rhyming Slang for 'fag', homosexual.

Toff – Upper class person.

Toffee Nosed – Upper class person.

Toilet Trader – Homosexual man.

Tom & Dick – Cockney Rhyming Slang for 'sick'.

Tom & Huck – Cockney Rhyming Slang for 'f*ck'.

Tom, Dick and Harry – Slang for everyone.

Tombola – Raffle.

Tom Cruise – Cockney Rhyming Slang for 'lose', 'booze', 'bruise'.

Tomfoolery – Cockney Rhyming Slang for 'jewelry'.

Tom Hanks – Cockney Rhyming Slang for 'thanks', 'Yanks'.

Tom Jones – Cockney Rhyming Slang for 'bones'.

Tom Kite – Cockney Rhyming Slang for 'shite'.

Tom Mix – Six.

Tommy - A British, usually English, soldier.

Tom Silk – Cockney Rhyming Slang for 'milk'.

Tom Tank – Cockney Rhyming Slang for 'wank', masturbate.

Tom Thumb – Cockney Rhyming Slang for 'bum', 'dumb'.

Tom Tit – Cockney Rhyming Slang for 'shit'.

Tommy Hilfiger – Cockney Rhyming Slang for 'nigger'.

Tommy Tank – Cockney Rhyming Slang for 'wank', masturbate.

Tommy Trinder – Cockney Rhyming Slang for 'window, (wind-er).

Tommy Tucker – Cockney Rhyming Slang for 'supper', also 'f*cker', 'f*ck her'.

Ton – A hundred.

Tonic – Cockney Rhyming Slang for 'Philharmonic'.

Tonsil Hockey – Kissing with deep tongues.

Tonsil Tennis – Kissing with deep tongues.

Tony Benn – Cockney Rhyming Slang for 'ten'. (origins; politician)

Tony Blair – Cockney Rhyming Slang for 'chair', 'hair''. (origins; Prime Minister)

Tony Slattery – Cockney Rhyming Slang for 'battery'. (origins; comedian)

Toodle Pip – A parting phrase, goodbye, WW2-ish.

Tool - Yet another word for your willy or penis. You'd think we were obsessed.

Tooting Bec – Cockney Rhyming Slang for 'peck', of food.

Top Banana – Top dog, top person.

Top Dollar – The very best price, good quality.

Top Hat – Cockney Rhyming Slang for 'chat'.

Top Hole – Toff exclamation of 'good', 'great'.

Topps Tiles – Cockney Rhyming Slang for 'piles', hemorrhoids.

Top Shag – The very best in a sexual partner.

Top Ten Hit – Cockney Rhyming Slang for 'shit'.

Top Totty – The very best looking girl/woman.

Top Whack - The very best price, good quality.

Top Yourself – Commit suicide.

Tord Gripps – Cockney Rhyming Slang for 'nips', nipples.

Tosh – Rubbish.

Tosser – A generic insult, also 'wanker', and shares the same hand signal.

Totty – Endearing slang for girl/woman.

Touching Cloth – In desperate need to defecate.

Touch Me on the Knob – Cockney Rhyming Slang for 'bob', shilling.

Town Crier – Cockney Rhyming Slang for 'liar'.

Town Halls – Cockney Rhyming Slang for 'balls', testicles.

Trackie – Track suit.

Tradesman's Entrance – The back door, sometimes used in a sexual way too.

Tramp on a Bench – Cockney Rhyming Slang for 'wench'.

Tramp Stamp – Tattoo on a woman.

Trashed – Drunk.

Trauchle – Scottish slang for trouble.

Treacle Tart – Cockney Rhyming Slang for 'sweetheart'.

Trevor Sinclair – Cockney Rhyming Slang for 'nightare'.

T-Rex – Cockney Rhyming Slang for 'text'. (origins; Pop Band)

Trolley – Shopping cart.

Trollied – Drunk.

Trombone – Cockney Rhyming Slang for 'phone'.

Trouble and Strife - Cockney Rhyming Slang for 'wife'.

Trouser Department – A man's sexual organs, penis and testicles. "He's quite endowed, you know, in the trouser department".

TTFN - Short for "ta ta for now", goodbye.

Tube of Glue – Cockney Rhyming Slang for 'clue'.

Tufnell Park – Cockney Rhyming Slang for 'lark'.

Tumble Down the Sink – Cockney Rhyming Slang for 'drink'.

Tumshie – Scottish slang for turnip, also a derogatory term, meaning idiot.

Tung Chee Hwa – Cockney Rhyming Slang for 'bra'.

Tuppence a Pound – Cockney Rhyming Slang for 'ground'.

Tuppence Ha'penny – Two and a half pennies, old money.

Turd Burglar – Gay man.

Turkish Bath – Cockney Rhyming Slang for 'laugh'.

Turkish Delight – Cockney Rhyming Slang for 'shite'.

Turtle Dove – Cockney Rhyming Slang for 'Love'.

Turtle Doves – Cockney Rhyming Slang for 'gloves'.

Turtle's Head - In desperate need to defecate.

Turn Up For the Books – An unusual/surprise happening or occurrence, usually a shock result.

Tutti Frutti – Cockney Rhyming Slang for 'beauty'. (origins; confectionery)

Twally – A stupid or dim person.

Twat – An idiot, also vagina, also to strike someone.

Twee - Dainty or quaint.

Twerp – Idiot.

Twig and Berries – Male sex organs.

Twist & Shout – Cockney Rhyming Slang for 'gout', 'kraut', German.

Twist & Twirl – Cockney Rhyming Slang for 'girl'.

Twit – Endearing slang for idiot. Short for 'nit-wit'.

Two & Eight – Cockney Rhyming Slang for 'state'.

Two & Six – Cockney Rhyming Slang for 'fix'.

Two Bob Bit – Cockney Rhyming Slang for 'shit'.

Two By Four – Cockney Rhyming Slang for 'draw'.

Two Fat Ladies – Eighty-Eight.

Two Finger Salute – Palm outward it means 'victory', used by Winston Churchill. Palm inward it means 'f*ck off'.

Two Little Ducks – Twenty two.

Two Thirty – Cockney Rhyming Slang for 'dirty'.

Twonk – Idiot.

Two Shakes of a Lamb's Tail – Means "a short time".

Tyne & Wear – Cockney Rhyming Slang for 'queer', homosexual.

Typewriter – Cockney Rhyming Slang for 'fighter'.

U IS FOR UNDER THE COSH

Umpteen – Means many, quite a few, more than ten, but after that, uncounted.

Uncle Ben – Cockney Rhyming Slang for 'ten'.

Uncle Bert – Cockney Rhyming Slang for 'shirt'.

Uncle Billy – Cockney Rhyming Slang for 'chilly'.

Uncle Bob – Cockney Rhyming Slang for 'job'.

Uncle Buck – Cockney Rhyming Slang for 'f*ck'.

Uncle Dick – Cockney Rhyming Slang for 'sick'.

Uncle Fester – Cockney Rhyming Slang for 'child molester'.

Uncle Fred – Cockney Rhyming Slang for 'bread'.

Uncle Gus – Cockney Rhyming Slang for 'bus'.

Uncle Ned – Cockney Rhyming Slang for 'bed', 'head'.

Uncle Reg – Cockney Rhyming Slang for 'veg', vegetables.

Uncles & Aunts – Cockney Rhyming Slang for 'pants', underwear.

Uncle Ted – Cockney Rhyming Slang for 'bed'.

Uncle Toby – Cockney Rhyming Slang for 'mobi', mobile phone.

Uncle Tom Cobley and All – From a song "Whitticombe Fair"… means everyone, everyone that's there.

Uncle Willie – Cockney Rhyming Slang for 'silly'.

Under the Cosh - An expression which means 'Under Pressure'.

Uni - Short for university, we would say we went to Uni like you would say you went to school or college.

Union Jack – Cockney Rhyming Slang for 'back'. (origins; British Flag)

Unscheduled Meeting – Cockney Rhyming Slang for 'a beating', assault.

Up a Gum Tree – In a situation which appears to have no solution to.

Up For It – Willing or eager to have sex.

Up the Duff – Means pregnant.

Up the Wooden hill to Bedford – Endearing slang for "Up the stairs to bed".

Up to Snuff – Up to a good standard.

Uri Gella – Cockney Rhyming Slang for 'Stella', pint of.

Use Your Loaf – Use your head, your intelligence or wit.

V IS FOR VAT

VAT – Value Added Tax.

Vanessa (Feltz) – Fifty Pounds (half a ton).

Vappy – Evaporated milk.

Vauxhall Cavalier – Cockney Rhyming Slang for 'queer', homosexual. (origins; British Car)

Vauxhall Novas – Cockney Rhyming Slang for 'Jehovah' (witness). (origins; British Car)

Veggie – Vegetarian.

Vera Lynn – Cockney Rhyming Slang for 'skin', 'gin'. (origins; singer)

Veronica Lake – Cockney Rhyming Slang for 'brake'.

Vexed – Anxious, stressed.

Vicar's Daughter – Cockney Rhyming Slang for 'quarter'.

Vincent Price – Cockney Rhyming Slang for 'ice'. (origins; actor)

Vincent van Gough – Cockney Rhyming Slang for 'cough', 'f*ck-off'. **(origins; Painter)**

Virginia Wades – Cockney Rhyming Slang for 'shades', sunglasses. (origins; tennis player)

Von Trappe – Cockney Rhyming Slang for 'crap'.

W IS FOR WINDOW LICKER

Wacky Backy - This is the stuff in a joint, otherwise known as pot or marijuana, grass, weed, ganja, cannabis.

Wad - Money, fist of paper money.

Waffle - To talk on and on about nothing.

Wag - To play truant, also Scottish for 'a bit of a player'.

Walking Papers – Slang for your termination documents, when you finish a job or get sacked, fired.

Wallace & Grommit – Cockney Rhyming Slang for 'vomit'. (origins; cartoon)

Wallup – To hit something.

Wally – Idiot.

Wally Grout – Cockney Rhyming Slang for 'shout', your time to buy drinks.

Walnut Whip – Cockney Rhyming Slang for 'trip', on drugs. (origins; confectionery)

Walter Anchor – Cockney Rhyming Slang for 'wanker'.

Walter Mitty – Cockney Rhyming Slang for 'kitty', titty'.

Wanger – Penis.

Wangle – To achieve a goal with guile, luck. "See Jimmy over there, he can wangle anything."

Wank – To masturbate.

Wanker - Derogatory term used to describe someone who is a bit of a jerk.

Wankers Cramp – Cockney Rhyming Slang for 'tramp'.

Wanking Chariot – Slang for your car, vehicle, could also be your bed.

Wankle – Loose, unsteady, shaky.

Warpaint – Make-up.

Washing-Up Liquid – Dish soap.

Watcha - Simply means Hi. Also short for "what do you" as in "watcha think of that"?

Watch & Chain – Cockney Rhyming Slang for 'brain'.

WC – Water Closet (toilet)

Watford Gap – Cockney Rhyming Slang for 'crap'.

Wayne Rooney – Cockney Rhyming Slang for 'loony'. (origins; footballer)

Wazz - To wee or pee.

Wazzock – Idiot.

Weasel & Stoat – Cockney Rhyming Slang for 'coat'.

Weaver's Chair – Cockney Rhyming Slang for 'prayer'.

Wee – To pee, also Scottish for 'small'.

Weed – Marijuana.

Weegie – A Glaswegian.

Weel Kent – Scottish slang for 'well known'.

Weeping Willow – Cockney Rhyming Slang for 'pillow'.

Well - Used to accentuate other words. Like "well hard" or "well good" or "well chuffed".

Welly – Big effort, force, also drunk.

Wedding Tackle – A man's sexual organs, meat and two veg, penis and testicles.

Wedge – Your stash of cash. Picture a pile of folded money; literally a wedge.

Weirsh – Scottish slang for bitter, sour, not tasting good.

Wellie (Welly) - It means you are trying harder or giving it the boot.

Wellied – Yup, yet another word for drunk. Just like the Eskimos have lots of words for snow, we do the same.

Wellies – Galoshes, short for 'Wellington Boots'.

Wendy House – A plastic tent in the shape of a house, for little girls to play in, with frame, and door etc.

West End Thespian – Cockney Rhyming Slang for 'lesbian'.

West Ham Reserves – Cockney Rhyming Slang for 'nerves'.

Westminster Abbey – Cockney Rhyming Slang for 'shabby'.

Westminster Bank – Cockney Rhyming Slang for 'wank', masturbate.

Weston Super-Mare – Cockney Rhyming Slang for 'nightmare'. (origins; town)

Wet & Wild – Cockney Rhyming Slang for 'child'.

Wet & Damp – Cockney Rhyming Slang for 'tramp'.

Wet Behind the Ears – A naïve, innocent, unexperienced person.

Wet Your Whistle - Have a drink, the first drink.

Whacked – Tired, exhausted.

Whatshisname – A person who's name can't be remembered.

Wheesht – Be quiet. (Haud yir wheesht) (Scottish)

Where It's At – A fashionable, good, popular place to be.

Whinge – To whine, complain.

Whisky & Soda – Cockney Rhyming Slang for 'Skoda', type of cheap car, also 'Voda', mobile phone.

Whistle & Flute – Cockney Rhyming Slang for 'suit'.

White Mice – Cockney Rhyming Slang for 'ice'.

Whole Kit and Kaboodle – Means; "Everything'. "He moved away, taking the whole kit and caboodle".

Whip Round – When people give money to a cause/person on the spur of the moment, when a crowd of tourists get together to give a 'collection' of cash to their driver, or a street performer, etc.

Whizz – Speed.

Wicked – Good, great, excellent.

Widdle – Pee, urinate.

Widow Twanky – Cockney Rhyming Slang for 'hanky'.

William Pitt – Cockney Rhyming Slang for 'shit'. (origins; Prime Minister)

Willies, The – A term for fear or fright. "He's scary; he gives me the willies".

Willy – Penis.

Willy Wonka – Cockney Rhyming Slang for 'plonker', idiot.

Wilson Picket – Cockney Rhyming Slang for 'ticket'.

Winch – Go steady with, go out with, date.

Wind & Kite – Cockney Rhyming Slang for 'web site'.

Wind Bag – A person who talks too much, a gas-bag.

Window Licker – A very derogatory term for the very handicapped. The term comes from their appearance on buses 'licking the windows'.

Wind up – To annoy someone, also a joke or prank.

Winnie the Pooh – Cockney Rhyming Slang for 'shoe'.

Wino – Homeless alcoholic.

Winona Ryder – Cockney Rhyming Slang for 'cyder'.

Wobbler - To have a tantrum, "Throw a wobbler".

Wobbly - To have a tantrum, "Throw a wobbler".

Wobbly Jelly – Cockney Rhyming Slang for 'telly', television.

Wog – An old/derogatory expression for a person of brown skin.

Wolf Your Food – To eat really fast, like a hungry dog or wolf.

Wonga – A slang term for 'cash' money.

Wonky - Shaky or unstable, also bent out of shape.

Wooden Pews – Cockney Rhyming Slang for 'news'.

Wooden Plank – Cockney Rhyming Slang for 'Yank'.

Woofter – Yet another word for homosexual, rhyming with 'poofter'.

Wooly Hat & Scarf – Cockney Rhyming Slang for 'laugh'.

Wooly Woofter – Cockney Rhyming Slang for 'poofter', homosexual.

Wormwood Scrubs – Cockney Rhyming Slang for 'pub'. (origins; Prison)

Worzel Gummidge – Cockney Rhyming Slang for 'rummage', 'scrummage'. (origins; kids tv)

Wotcher – A general greeting of hello.

Wrigley's Gum – Cockney Rhyming Slang for 'bum'.

Wrinkly (Wrinklies) – A rather descriptive term for 'old people', dealing with their wrinkly skin rather than other, more lofty, attributes.

Wuss – Weak person.

Wyatt Earp – Cockney Rhyming Slang for 'burp'.

Y IS FOR YOU'RE HAVING A LAUGH

Yakking - This means talking incessantly - not that I know anyone who does that now!

Yarmouth Bloater – Cockney Rhyming Slang for 'motor', car.

Yob – A hooligan, a trouble-looking youth, ned, idiot.

Yogi Bear – Cockney Rhyming Slang for 'hair'.

Yonks – Ages, a considerable time, years. "Blimey, I haven't heard from you for yonks".

You & Me – Cockney Rhyming Slang for 'cup of tea'.

You Get Me? – Do you understand?

You Must – Cockney Rhyming Slang for 'crust'.

You're Having a Laugh – Means; "You're joking, right?"

YoYo Ma – Cockney Rhyming Slang for 'car'.

Yul Brynner – Cockney Rhyming Slang for 'dinner'. (origins; actor)

Yuri Geller – Cockney Rhyming Slang for 'Stella', beer.

Z IS FOR ZACHARY SCOTTS

Zachary Scotts – Cockney Rhyming Slang for 'trots', diarrhea.

Zed - The last letter of the alphabet.

Zig & Zag – Cockney Rhyming Slang for 'shag'.

Zippy & Bungle – Cockney Rhyming Slang for 'jungle'.

Zonked - Totally knackered, exhausted.

That's it.

We hope that you enjoyed our dictionary, and found it useful, informative, amusing or all three.

If we've missed your own particular slang favorite, we apologize, and offer our email address for you to contact us with your own blockbuster.

www.ianhallauthor@gmail.com

Thank you all again.

Ian Hall

2016

Printed in Great Britain
by Amazon